PRECIOUS CARGO
SCOTS AND THE CHINA TRADE

蘇中貿易

Susan Leiper

N·M·S

NATIONAL
MUSEUMS OF
SCOTLAND
PUBLISHING

Foreword

Cable & Wireless is delighted to sponsor *Precious Cargo*. The company has a long history of involvement with trade with China, dating from 1871 when the first British telegraph cable was laid from the UK to Hong Kong.

For 125 years, Cable & Wireless has provided telecommunications services, networks and equipment to business and residential customers around the world. There are Cable & Wireless businesses in the UK, Europe, the Caribbean, Australia and the Far East. Hongkong Telecom, which is a Cable & Wireless subsidiary, has an excellent reputation for the quality of its communications services, and has helped make Hong Kong such a major business centre in the Pacific Rim region.

International trade in the modern era depends on fast, reliable communications which are the business of Cable & Wireless. We hope that readers of this book and visitors to the accompanying exhibition will gain an insight into the history of trading links between Scotland and the vast, fascinating country of China.

Dr N Brian Smith CBE
Chairman, Cable and Wireless plc

With additional help from the Russell Trust

Designed and published by National Museums of Scotland Publishing,
Chambers Street, Edinburgh EH1 1JF
© NMS Publishing 1997

British Library Cataloguing in Publication Data
A catalogue record of this book is available from the British Library

ISBN 0 948636 90 4
Printed by South Sea International Press Ltd in Hong Kong

Cover: *Chinese porcelain plate painted with two Scotsmen, about 1745, and Chinese embroidered satin wall hanging made for export in the 19th century.*

Frontispiece: *Some of the trading factories on the Canton waterfront, on James Drummond's wallpaper. The absence of the American flag and the architecture of the buildings date the wallpaper to about 1780. The flags identify the factories as, from left to right: French, Swedish and British.*

Contents

1
Early days

MADE IN CHINA. Not many of us get through a day without encountering something bearing that label. It may no longer be our breakfast tea or the cup we drink it out of, but it may be our electric kettle, our socks, our soy sauce or a colour-printed book like this one. We take all these for granted. We seldom question where they come from. Yet all these things, and a multitude more, are the result of over three centuries of trade with China and subsequently Hong Kong.

The impact of the Scots on the China trade has been enormous. For most of us the China trade means exotic silks and pretty china, which undoubtedly brought a touch of luxury to the lives of those who could afford them. What is less well known is that there was a busy trade in more practical, everyday items such as tea, medicinal drugs, plants, dyestuffs and food-stuffs. It is with these commodities that the Scottish connection is strongest. In many cases the Chinese silks, porcelain and knick-knacks that we associate with the trade were merely by-products of a trade in necessities.

The Scots have always had a name for them-selves as explorers. Even today on a dreich winter morning in Scotland who would not be tempted to drift on a riverboat through a Chinese landscape or sample the lively bustle of Hong Kong? At the end of the sixteenth century, William Carmichael, who is credited as being the first British visitor to Macau on the southern coast of China, was certainly touched by a spirit of adventure. And he was a Scot.

Carmichael may have been an adventurer, but he was not a trader. At the time he visited

Colonial-style houses in Macau, painted, as John Thomson described others in the 1870s, 'in a variety of strange colours'.

The Bay of Macau from the North *by George Chinnery, about 1830 (detail). The Portuguese flag is hoisted at the end of the Praya Grande.*

China few Scots or even British had any knowledge of such far-flung lands as China, let alone any desire to trade with them. The importance of William Carmichael's visit to Macau lies more in what he would have seen there, and the inkling he may have had of how a European nation might coexist and trade with a country that offered goods of a very desirable nature.

Macau is a small hilly peninsula not far from the better known centres of Canton (nowadays known as Guangzhou) and Hong Kong. It was here that the earliest European maritime traders with China, the Portuguese, decided to settle in 1556, as Macau provided a convenient anchorage and a pleasant place to live. Ever since Vasco da Gama's discovery of the west coast of India in 1498 and the subsequent establishment in 1510 of Goa as the Portuguese centre of trade in the east, the Portuguese had been gradually pushing eastwards in their search for new lands and new goods. They were encouraged to do so as a result of the closure of the eastern Mediterranean by the Ottoman Turks. By the time the Portuguese reached Malacca on the west coast of what is now Peninsular Malaysia they were beginning to hear tales of a mysterious people known as the Chin who occupied a vast land even further to the east. As the Chin, or Chinese as we know them, had since 1431 been forbidden by their emperors to make any more overseas trading expeditions (they had previously ventured as far west as Africa), it was left to the Portuguese to try and gain control of local trade in the eastern seas. This they began tentatively by trading illegally between Malacca, China and Japan, but by 1555 they had ingratiated themselves sufficiently with the Chinese to be allowed to make seasonal visits to Canton where they paid the required taxes and traded openly.

From Lisbon the Portuguese ships, known as carracks, brought metalware, cut glass, mirrors, clocks and, presumably for the use of the Portuguese themselves, wine. En route for Macau the ships picked up other commodities in Goa and Malacca: Indian cotton, Middle Eastern jewellery and daggers, and spices from the Celebes (now Sulawesi). Trade with the east was by no means a simple two-way affair: there was a lot of picking up and dropping off on the way. By topping up these goods with silver bullion from their recently acquired colonies in South America, the Portuguese bought from the Chinese not only porcelain and silk, but also the miniature oranges known as kumquats, ginger and medicinal drugs such as rhubarb root. These they shipped both to Lisbon and to other parts of Asia.

It was in Lisbon that William Carmichael would have encountered these goods and the stories of eastern peoples. Carmichael's spirit of adventure had taken him on a ship from Scotland to Lisbon in 1579, and from there, two years later, to Goa where he served in the government for thirty years. It was during this period that he visited Macau, though sadly he was never to return to Scotland to tell of Portugal's successes there. Having deserted his post in Goa in 1611, Carmichael moved on to the Dutch Celebes where he was imprisoned as a spy. On his release he returned to London where he tried unsuccessfully to gain compensation for his maltreatment by the Dutch. He failed and was destined to end his eventful life in a poorhouse.

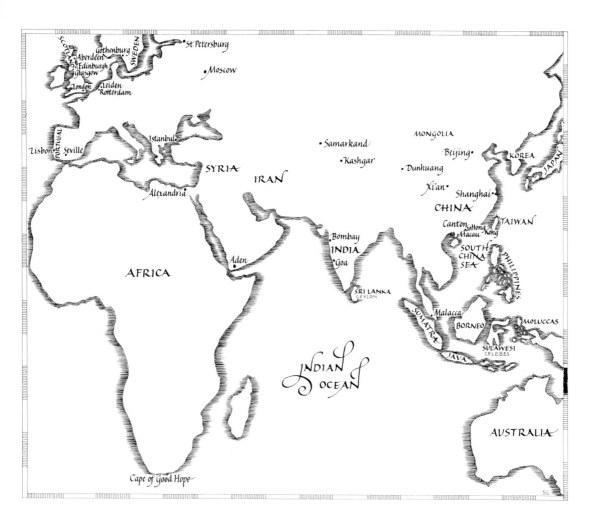

He would of course have had a story to tell back in England, as would some of the other British sailors who had joined the crews of Portuguese ships but who remain untraceable because they took Portuguese names. Such stories were substantiated in 1591 when a Portuguese carrack was captured and brought in to harbour at Plymouth. Its amazing cargo from all over Asia, consisting of jewels, spices, medicinal drugs, silks, calicoes, carpets, porcelain and ivory, must have caused confusion as to the origin of the goods, but it was enough to whet the appetites of British traders. Furthermore, the construction of the carrack itself provided an important lesson for British shipwrights.

Portuguese skill in shipbuilding and navigation was really the key to their success as the first European maritime traders with China. Not only did these skills get them to China in the first place, but they so impressed the Chinese in Macau that there was an

Portuguese Carracks off a
Rocky Coast *in the style of
Joachim Patinir, about 1500.*

*Chinese trading junk from
Fujian province, on James
Drummond's wallpaper, about
1780. Note the similarity to a
Portuguese carrack.*

instant rapport between the two peoples. Chinese coastal traders from Fujian province who came regularly to Canton and Macau sailed junks not unlike Portuguese carracks in their construction. The Fujianese were therefore able to help maintain the Portuguese ships. As both seafaring peoples shared an appetite for fish, the Fujianese were further able to assist the Portuguese in Macau by supplying them with seafood. Such was Portuguese navigational skill that they were also adept at suppressing piracy off the south China coast, which of course raised their standing in the eyes of the Chinese. The Portuguese presence in Macau was therefore of benefit to the Chinese, and through their amicable relationship the Portuguese gained a monopoly of the China trade until the end of the sixteenth century.

One of the conveniences of the history of the China trade is the neatness with which it can be roughly divided into centuries. The sixteenth century saw the dominance of the Portuguese, which gave way to Dutch control in the seventeenth century and finally to British supremacy in the eighteenth and nineteenth centuries. This is of course a sweeping generalization, but one that serves as a useful outline for the story.

With Portugal's independence weakened by her union with Spain in 1580, Portuguese possessions in the east were soon forcibly taken over by the Dutch. By the time the Dutch had gained control of the China trade at the beginning of the seventeenth century, the involvement of the Scots, albeit in a circuitous way, may have been greater than has hitherto been realized. The Dutch were well aware of what China had to offer from their regular traffic with the Portuguese capital, Lisbon. In the first few years of the seventeenth century their interest had been stimulated by the capture of several Portuguese carracks and the sale of their cargoes in the Netherlands. At this time trade between Scotland and the Netherlands was flourishing, the Scots having an authorized trading station at Veere on the island of Zeeland. From the 1640s Rotterdam was to become the principal port for trade with Scotland. Many Scottish merchants sent their sons there to serve apprenticeships, and a large community of Scots grew up in the city. Surely these Scots must have been aware of what was coming into Amsterdam and Zeeland from China?

We know for certain, because his letters have survived, that a Scotsman, Andrew Russell from Stirling, was the factor for Scottish trade in Rotterdam from 1668 to 1695 and that among the many things he sent to his numerous correspondents in Scotland were garden seeds, medicinal drugs and linen cloth, some of which might have originated in China. It is tempting to speculate how many of his unspecified 'small matted bundells' and boxes contained goods from China.

The mention of medicinal drugs is important, both in the context of the Scottish-Dutch connection and in relation to our next important Scottish visitor to China: Dr John Bell of Antermony near Kirkintilloch in Stirlingshire. Unlike William Carmichael who witnessed Portuguese maritime trade with China from Macau, John Bell was to approach China from the north, from St Petersburg in Russia, following a passage somewhat parallel to that of the ancient Silk Route. This overland route from the west of China to the Mediterranean had been the principal trade route from China to the west and back again from very early times. By the fourteenth century belligerent foreign powers on China's northern and western borders had put a stop to overland trade, and attention turned to China's growing southern ports and maritime trade.

Like Carmichael, Dr Bell was not a trader. Rather he was a qualified physician with 'a strong desire of seeing foreign parts' and a knack of recording them. In 1714, at the age

John Bell's route from Moscow to Beijing, published in his Travels *of 1763.*

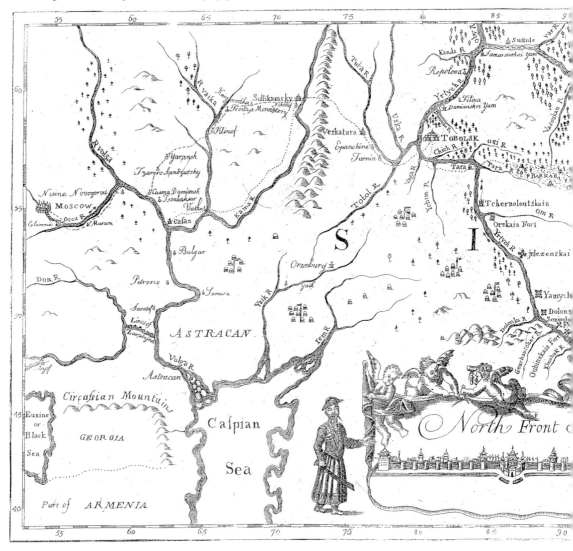

of twenty-three, he went to St Petersburg to be assistant to Dr Areskine, physician to Tsar Peter the Great. After initial service on an embassy to Persia, Bell joined a second embassy in 1719, this time from St Petersburg to Beijing (or Pekin as he calls it). On his return to Scotland some twenty years later, Bell so amused his friends with tales of his travels that he was persuaded to rewrite his journals along the lines of *Gulliver's Travels*, calling his own work *Travels from St Petersburg in Russia to Diverse Parts of Asia*. One can

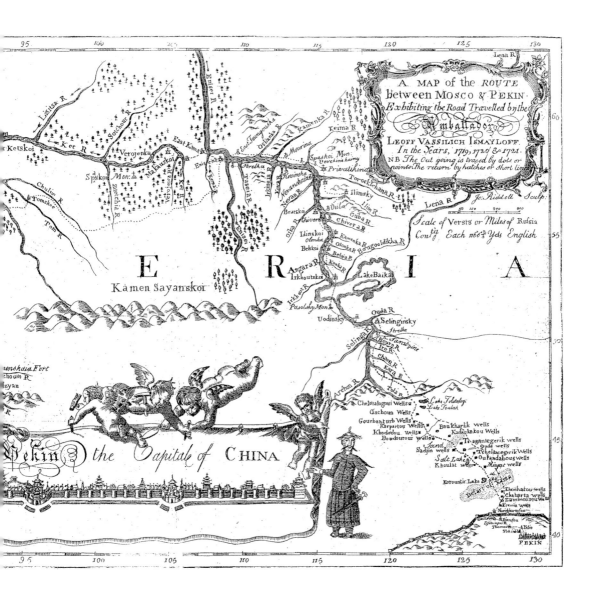

imagine how Bell's stories would have enthralled his friends when they were published in 1763, and today they still provide a tantalizing early account of a Scot's impressions in northern China.

The party of sixty men and women travelled for sixteen months, riding first by sleigh through Siberia, then on camel and horseback into China. At one point they had to swim across a river that was frozen in places; on another occasion they passed through countryside ravaged by a recent earthquake, 'a dismal scene to see', and shortly afterwards the chief cook 'dropped down . . . and immediately expired'. However, hardships were balanced by high points: one evening they found fresh running water and lit a fire to broil mutton chops which were washed down not just with fresh water but also with 'burgundy and champaign' (which someone must have had the forethought to provide). As they approached China it was decided to send the women home rather than wait for six weeks for a 'special order from the Emperor' to admit them. Bell was told by a cautious Chinese that there 'had never been an European woman in China' and this particular Chinese 'could not be answerable for introducing the first'.

The length and rigours of the trip must have unhinged one member of the party, for, at the sight of the Great Wall he called out 'Land!' Once through a gate in the wall 'Everything now appeared to us as if we had arrived in another world', a world of high rocky mountains and little scattered cottages, with spots of cultivated ground 'much resembling those romantick . . . landskips which are painted on the CHINA-ware . . . of this country. These are accounted fanciful by most EUROPEANS, but are really natural'. (Note Bell's use of the term CHINA-ware, in its original sense of 'ware from China'. This of course became shortened to china, denoting the material, which serves as a reminder of the impact made by Chinese porcelain on our domestic lives.) From now on the ambassador and his entourage were 'guests' of the Chinese emperor 'who entertains all ambassadors, and bears their expenses'.

A guard of five hundred Chinese horsemen cleared the way for the party's entry to Beijing and Bell says 'One would have imagined all the people in PEKIN were assembled to see us.' Naturally the Chinese were as amazed to stare at this foreign embassy as Bell was to observe the Chinese. His stay of three months in Beijing from December 1720 to March 1721 was not short of spectacles. Bell attended the court ceremony when the Russian ambassador met the ageing Kangxi emperor, who had reigned for almost sixty years. The emperor sat cross-legged on his throne and, in response to gifts of furs, clocks and repeating watches, sent the embassy delicacies from his own table on massive gold dishes. The luxury of the numerous banquets, eaten with 'a couple of ivory-pins', impressed Bell (on one occasion they were served sturgeon that had been transported from Russia encased in snow), although the almost complete absence of liquor was also worthy of note! Bell visited the emperor's stables with its elephants 'only for show', the emperor's 'glass-house' (the first in China), the observatory, a porcelain manufactory and even a market where he was somewhat taken aback to see a dozen dead badgers in the butcher's shop. But, despite his horror at the Chinese practices of tiger-baiting and foot-binding, and the 'shocking and unnatural practice' of abandoning new-born infants in the streets overnight, Bell found the Chinese 'civilized and hospitable' and 'complaisant to strangers'. Above all he praised 'their regard for their parents, and decent treatment of their women of all ranks'.

John Bell was not short of tales. But his writings disclose a chance encounter that was to have an enormous impact on medical and botanical research in Scotland over the following seventy years. One morning Bell left his tent and climbed to the top of a hill 'where I found many plants of excellent rhubarb; and, by the help of a stick, dug up as much of it as I wanted'. This he took back to St Petersburg.

For most of us today rhubarb means rhubarb crumble, rhubarb and ginger jam, and the profusion of pink stems concealed beneath large green leaves in a neglected corner of the garden. But this species of rhubarb has only been cultivated and used in the kitchen for about two hundred years. Until around 1800 rhubarb root from foreign sources had quite a different use: it cured constipation. It was a medicinal drug, not a sweetmeat. And as far as the Chinese were concerned, in terms of trade, medicinal rhubarb was indispensable to the British: 'The foreigners from the West are naturally fond of milk, and cream; indulgence in these luxuries induces costiveness, when there is nothing but rhubarb and tea that will clear their system and restore their spirits.'

The use of rhubarb root as a medicinal drug has a long history. The dried and cured root of a species of rhubarb related to, but different from, our garden rhubarb had been used by the Chinese, the Greeks and the Romans. It was probably reintroduced to Europe in the Middle Ages by the Arabs who were already trading with the east. The appearance of foreign medi-

The plant which produces the best medicinal rhubarb root: Rheum palmatum.

True Rhubarb from John Parkinson's Theater of Plantes *of 1646. Parkinson blamed the English weather for the fact that this type of rhubarb, which he grew in his garden in Longacre in London, was a less efficient laxative than that imported from China.*

cinal drugs led to the revival of classical herbals which described the growth and use of herbs and medicinal drugs. In turn the demand for medicinal drugs gave rise to the apothecary who dealt both in medicinal drugs and spices. Medicine and food went hand in hand, and the need for storage necessitated containers. We shall see exactly the same pattern with another great medicinal plant, tea, which bred its own paraphernalia of equipment and boosted trade.

Rhubarb had always been considered foreign. Its early name *Rha barbarum* suggests a remote, even barbaric, source, and its many later names – Russia, Turkey, China rhubarb – all derive from the places from which it was believed to have come. Eventually it was discovered that the best rhubarb was the species with broad segmented leaves like an outstretched palm, hence its name *Rheum palmatum*. The best source of this plant was Gansu province in the far northwest of China, which lay on the ancient Silk Route. When the root was dried it was solid, yellow on the outside, and variegated inside like a nutmeg, with reddish streaks.

John Bell's vital role in the search for the best rhubarb was not recognized until 1792, seventy years after his travels in China. In that year a fellow Scot, Sir William Fordyce, wrote: 'Though it has long been known, as a valuable article of commerce between Russia, Turkey, Persia, China, and England, it was left for Mr Bell of Antermony, a Scotch gentleman . . . to inform us particularly where it was first discovered.' Bell's description of the rhubarb seeds being scattered by marauding marmots is rather quaint, as is his account of how the Mongols cut the root into small pieces, threaded a cord through the middle of each, and then hung them 'about their tents, and sometimes on the horns of their sheep'. Bell justified his dwelling on the 'growth and management of the rhubarb' with the excuse that he had never read 'a satisfactory account where, or how, it grows'. He believed it could be easily cultivated. And how right he was!

Who would have believed that Britain and, in particular, Scotland, was on the verge of being gripped by a veritable rhubarb-growing craze? For Scotland this phenomenon was not entirely outlandish. By the early years of the eighteenth century, when Bell was visiting China, Scotland was undergoing an unprecedented medical boom, partly due to her links with the University of Leiden in the Netherlands, which at that time was the centre of medical research in Europe. Again we are witnessing the strength of ties between Scotland and the Netherlands. The great professor of medicine and botany at Leiden, Herman Boerhaave, was influential in the development of the Edinburgh medical school, having trained not only the first professor of medicine and botany at Edinburgh but also a number of subsequent ones. Although the combination of medicine and botany was not a new one, it demonstrated the importance of botanical research in the hunt for efficient remedies for medical conditions.

Boerhaave took a great deal of interest in the physic or botanic garden in Leiden, and by the 1660s leading physicians in Edinburgh had established two physic gardens in the city. So the atmosphere was ripe for experimentation with the seeds of a foreign plant such as rhubarb. Boerhaave grew rhubarb, and in 1753 a new kind of rhubarb seed, probably from the same species of plant that Bell had discovered, arrived in St Petersburg from China and was grown successfully there by Russia's director general of medicine, a Scot and friend of Bell, Dr Mounsey. On Mounsey's retirement in 1762 he brought back some seeds of the successful rhubarb plants to Scotland and distributed them amongst his Scottish friends. Of these Dr John Hope, professor of medicine and botany, pioneered the cause of cultivating the best rhubarb in Britain to prevent 'the sending out . . . to foreign parts, great sums of money for this article of commerce'.

With a similar aim, the Society of Arts chose rhubarb as a product worthy of promotion, and in the second half of the eighteenth century awarded more medals for the successful growth in Britain of rhubarb than for any other agricultural product except the

The two most important medicinal drugs imported from China: dried rhubarb root and dried China root.

dye plant madder. One of these medals went, in 1793, to Sir William Fordyce who had grown plants originating from Mounsey's seed, and had dried the roots successfully. The dried roots were then ground to a powder and mixed with a variety of other substances to create a cure for constipation. Dr James Gregory, professor of medicine at the University of Edinburgh in the late eighteenth century, was to mix powdered rhubarb root with powdered ginger and magnesium to create the famous Gregory's Powder which was a common remedy for constipation until well into this century. This, or

Edinburgh pharmacist's order book, 1846-56. Note that on the same day both Mr Bevin and Miss Gordon have prescriptions containing Rhei pal. (powdered rhubarb root), and Miss Gordon also has sarsaparilla, another name for China root.

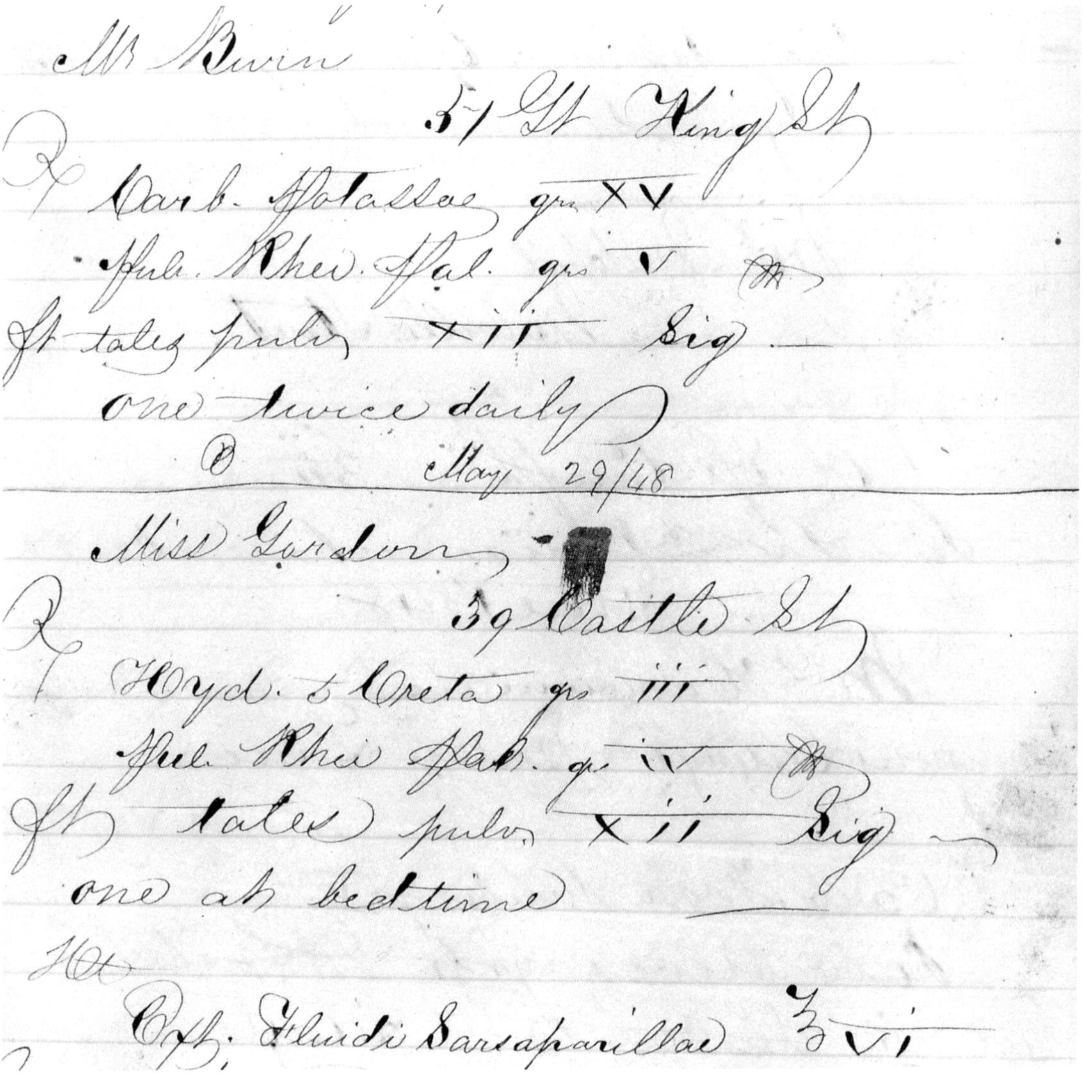

Mr Bevin

57 Gt King St

℞ Carb. Potassae gr. XV

Pul. Rhei. Pal. gr. V (℞)

Ft tales pulv. XII Sig

one twice daily

May 29/48

Miss Gordon

39 Castle St

℞ Hyd. c Creta gr. iii

Pul. Rhei. Pal. gr. iv (℞)

Ft tales pulv. XII Sig

one at bedtime

℞ Ext. Fluid. Sarsaparillae ℥vi

18

something similar, is what Elizabeth Grant of Rothiemurchus describes in her *Memories of a Highland Lady*, written in the mid-nineteenth century. The daily diet was so inadequate that 'the rhubarb bottle became a necessary appendage in the nursery'.

The 1790s saw the cultivation of British rhubarb and the use of home-grown roots in Edinburgh and other leading hospitals reach their peak. Yet shortly after this time commercial plantings of rhubarb and the Society of Art's support of it began to decline. Perhaps the British climate or soil, or the curing methods used, could not produce rhubarb roots of a quality equal to those imported from China. This however was good for the China trade. For despite the rhubarb-growing craze in Britain in the second half of the eighteenth century, the search for the source of the best foreign rhubarb was continuing, and rhubarb root was being imported in considerable quantities from China. At this point we must leave the British rhubarb story and Dutch ties with Scotland, and turn the clock back again to the beginning of the eighteenth century to see how British involvement in the China trade was growing.

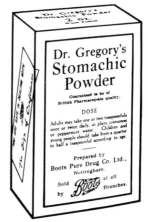

Boots patent brand of Dr Gregory's Stomachic Powder, 1932.

The prescription for Gregory's Powder, in James Gregory's own handwriting. Pulvaris Rhei palmati *is powdered rhubarb root.*

2
The East India Company

The rhubarb-growing craze of the eighteenth century ran concurrently with an enormous upsurge in the export of medicinal drugs from China to Britain. Another popular drug was China root, sometimes known as sarsaparilla, which, like rhubarb root, was powdered and used in cures for colds, headaches, gout and syphilis. But as the British gradually took over from the Dutch as the main traders with China in the eighteenth century, their success was to centre on what was initially considered another plant with medicinal properties, and one which was to have a far greater impact than rhubarb. This was tea.

Compared with rhubarb root, tea was a fairly late arrival on the scene in Europe, although it had been popular in China since at least the seventh century. In 1658 a London coffee house advertised 'that excellent, and by all Physicians approved, *China* Drink, called by the *Chineans, Tcha,* and by other nations *Tay alias Tee*'. Samuel Pepys drank his first 'Cupp of Tee (a China drink)' in 1660, and by the 1690s there are occasional references to tea drinking in Scotland, although only amongst the upper classes.

We know from the detailed account books kept by Lady Grisell Baillie, who married a Whig member of parliament in 1691 and lived in Edinburgh before moving in 1707 to her husband's family seat at Mellerstain in Berwickshire, that she ordered both black and green teas and had a fashionable 'japan Tee Table', furnished with kettle, teapot, stoup, basin, 'litle green Tee cups and sassers' and 'a pot for milk to tee'. Already we have evidence of the British fashion for milk and sugar in tea, making quite a different drink from the unadulterated infusion drunk by the Chinese. Perhaps the British required a drink with more body, accustomed as they were to beer and ale as their basic beverages. As tea drinking began in coffee houses, the addition of milk to tea may have seemed the natural parallel to milk with coffee. Lady Baillie's first recorded purchase of tea is in 1708, when she buys half a pound of Bohea (black tea from the Bohea mountains in south-eastern China) at about £2 a pound. In 1710 she adds an order for a quarter pound of green tea at about £1 a pound. By 1715 she appears to be buying tea from local merchants (Lewis Pringle, Mr Blair, Gilbert Pringle) and extending her repertoire to Beco (Pekoe) and a 'fine green Tee cal'd Heyson Tee at fergison'. These merchants may have procured their tea from London, via the East India Company, but it is equally likely that there was a direct trade in tea between Scotland and the Netherlands as in 1716 Lady Baillie purchases eight pounds of tea from Holland and another eight pounds from 'Mr Jerrard at Raterdam [Rotterdam]'.

Whampoa by E Duncan, after W J Huggins (detail). Ships such as the East Indiaman flying a British flag would have remained anchored at Whampoa for three or four months while the supercargoes went to Canton.

Fou lin.

The plant which produces China root, from Du Halde's General History of China *of 1736.*

When compared with the very low price of both beer and ale at the time, tea was expensive, although Lady Baillie also spent quite a bit on two other drugs from China: rhubarb root and China root or sarsaparilla. In its early days tea was certainly regarded as a luxury, being stored in locking tea caddies to prevent its consumption by the servants. In fact Lady Baillie's directions to her servants in 1743 mention only beer for the servants, while one of their daily duties is to 'Have tea, water and what may be usualy cald for in the afternoon ready'.

The tax levied on tea added to its cost. As a consequence tea smuggling became big business, particularly in Scotland. With its regular trade with the Netherlands and the Scandinavian countries already in place, Scotland was well suited to this parallel but illicit trade. Large walled farms were built on coastal sites and travellers engaged to distribute the tea. The low cost of this smuggled tea may explain why some Highlanders could afford to drink 'Dutch' tea, often with the addition of a little cinnamon – another trade item from the east – and sometimes a dash of whisky.

However, as tea consumption rose dramatically in the eighteenth century, its price fell steadily, and by the 1770s the average price was about five shillings (twenty-five pence) a pound. When in 1784 the tea tax was reduced substantially, partly because high grain prices were affecting the cost and quality of beer and ale, tea had become an economical substitute for beer and ale and was fast becoming the national drink.

But what had caused the British to be interested in tea in the first place? Portuguese traders in the sixteenth century wrote home about tea but do not appear to have exported much. By the middle of the following century the Portuguese must have developed a taste for the drink because it is said that when Catherine of Braganza came from Portugal to England in 1662 to marry Charles II she helped to stimulate the fashion for tea drinking. The Dutch were beginning to ship tea via Java by the beginning of the seventeenth century, and by the 1650s a good deal of tea was being sold by apothecaries in the Netherlands. This outlet suggests that it was considered to have medicinal properties, which were highlighted by the Dutchman Jan Nieuhoff after his visit to China on an embassy in 1655 when he wrote that tea could drive away drowsiness, aid digestion, counteract an excess of alcohol, prevent gout and gallstones and promote the powers of memory. With such a wealth of promised benefits perhaps it is little wonder that tea drinking caught on.

The words used for tea in European languages give an insight into where each country procured its tea. The Portuguese use *cha*, derived from the Cantonese *cha*, showing, as expected, that they shipped their tea from Macau and Canton where the Cantonese dialect is spoken. The Dutch use *thea* and the English 'tea', both derived from *te*, the Chinese dialect spoken around Amoy (present-day Xiamen) and the island of Chusan (p46) where the English made their early attempts to establish trading bases. The English 'cup o' char' must have grown out of later contact with Canton where they were eventually to establish their trading base.

A trading base at Canton, as the Portuguese had achieved at Macau, was of course what British traders were after. In their initial eagerness to match Portuguese and Dutch successes in the spice trade, the British had, in 1600, established a company to trade with the East Indies, although neither East nor Indies meant much to the London merchants involved at the time. Sporadic success followed in the Moluccas, and the company set up headquarters in India. In the early 1630s a few British ships were permitted by the Portuguese to trade from Macau, but the first official British traders to China in 1637 were rebuffed by the Chinese. The ships nevertheless returned to London loaded with green ginger, loose gold, China root, tubs of porcelain, chests of cloves and gold chains, but no tea. In 1676 the British managed to procure bases at Chusan and Amoy, which were ideally situated in their proximity to the major tea and silk producing regions of China, but these were not to last.

Squabbles within the British trading company led to the establishment of a rival faction. Rivalry stimulated the desire to gain a foothold in China, and in 1709 the two rival companies joined forces to become the East India Company. By 1711 this company had established a firm trading base at Canton, from where it was to dominate European trade with China throughout the eighteenth century. So firm was the company's monopoly of trade with China that any Scot who was involved in this trade would automatically have been attached to an East Indiaman, the type of ship used by the company. And we know that a huge number of Scots *were* employed by the East India Company. Some were eager to escape the political upheavals at home. Others, as we might expect from their involvement in the rhubarb-growing craze, were enthusiastic medical practitioners, keen to try their hand as ship's physicians and botanical collectors. One

Life in a rural Chinese village, on James Drummond's wallpaper.

Scot, James Drummond, was to rise to the position of President of the Select Committee responsible for the dealings of the East India Company in Canton.

When he retired to Perthshire in 1812, Drummond brought back with him rolls of magnificent handpainted Chinese wallpaper which were later pasted to the walls of his upstairs drawing room. On entering the room, the elderly James Drummond would have delighted guests by showing them, on the left, a complete sweep of the trading factories on the Canton waterfront (frontispiece), before sitting round the fire to admire scenes of Chinese agriculture, village life, snack shops, acrobats and children playing. This wallpaper gives us a marvellous impression of what the average East India Company employee would have seen and experienced on his trips to China. It also provides an insight into the trading system at Canton.

The city of Canton with its tall pagoda and Chinese officials on horseback is clearly separated from the row of elegant western-style buildings lining the busy Pearl River waterfront. These, each with its identifying flag, are the European trading houses, which are more commonly referred to as factories or *hongs*. (The China trade supports a barrage of idiosyncratic vocabulary which, when its origins are elucidated, adds to an understanding of the trading system.) The word factory comes from the Portuguese *feitoria*, an agent's office, and *hong* from the Cantonese for a trade or house of business. However, the factories were more than just offices for the foreign traders: they incorporated ground-floor warehouses and residential apartments above. The row of factories was quite short, each nation having only a narrow frontage, but each building stretching back about 300 metres to abut the suburbs of Canton (p51). Foreigners were restricted to the factory area, as is indicated on the wallpaper where the only two foreigners are conversing on the quay in front of the Swedish factory.

As far as the western trader was concerned, life in the China trade was fraught with restrictions: he was allowed to trade only from Canton, and only from the factory area; he was permitted to go to Canton only in the trading season from October to March, after which he had to retire to Macau for the summer; he was not allowed to take his wife into Canton; and his leisure pursuits consisted of drinking imported European wine with his colleagues in the luxury of the factory dining room, getting drunk on a Chinese concoction of alcohol, tobacco juice, sugar and arsenic peddled in the back streets by Chinese hawkers, or spending a risky night on a 'flower' boat or in a red pavilion. Restrictions were also imposed on the trader's daily business, when he was forced to communicate via a Chinese interpreter, often in a hotchpotch language composed of pidgin English, Chinese and Portuguese, with the Chinese merchant allotted to him.

These *hong* merchants are usually identifiable by the suffix -qua, a term of respect, which was added to their names. Hence we meet Mowqua, Tenqua, Howqua and many more. The *hong* merchants were organized into a cooperative of thirteen, known as the Cohong, which was responsible for the behaviour of foreign merchants in Canton, and for making sure that European traders did not attempt to deal with smaller Chinese merchants whose goods might have been cheaper.

There were shipping restrictions too. When an East Indiaman arrived at Macau, at the mouth of the Pearl River, her captain had to report to Chinese customs, pay an entry fee and hire a

The prosperous Chinese hong merchant Howqua, who was renowned for his beautiful garden in Canton. His sunken features suggest a propensity for opium smoking.

pilot to guide her through the Bogue (or Tiger's Mouth as it was more colourfully known) and on up to the island of Whampoa, not far from Canton, where the ship was forced to anchor as the river became too shallow further up. From Whampoa the officer known as the supercargo (from the Portuguese *sobrecarga*), who was responsible for overseeing the ship's cargo and its sale, would proceed to the Canton factories in a small boat, leaving the members of his crew behind to get hot and bored in the confines of the ship that they already knew intimately after six to nine months at sea.

All these restrictions, understandably, irked the British traders. But frustration was to simmer for more than half a century before an attempt was made to rectify the situation. One reason for this tardiness may have been the fact that, despite restrictions, the second half of the eighteenth century saw an insatiable appetite in Europe for things Chinese and an enormous boom in trade with China. Tea was the principal item of export from China and it was to stimulate the export of other goods. Tea tables like Lady Grisell Baillie's required teapots, cups, saucers, milk jugs and sugar basins, many of which were first made in Britain of silver or other metals. But if the Chinese could make them out of porcelain, and more cheaply too, then why not order a whole dinner service, complete, if you ranked in the upper echelons of society, with your coat of arms? Thus developed the fashion for sets of Chinese armorial porcelain.

Tea's lighter-weight partner in the ship's cargo was silk, whose export had a further impact on the porcelain trade. Ships carrying tea and silk required ballast in their bilges to ensure their stability. Porcelain was the perfect solution. Moreover it acted as a water-proof lining to protect the more perishable teas and silks from seawater, rain and condensation.

Chinese porcelain had appealed originally to the Portuguese and Dutch traders in the sixteenth and early seventeenth centuries because it was so attractive: freely executed patterns and lively scenes of Chinese life painted in vivid blue on a glazed white ground. It was also very strong. No porcelain was being made in the west at this time, and yet the Chinese had been mass-producing it for centuries at centres such as Jingdezhen in southern China and elsewhere. The Dutch began to import blue and white wares *en*

Chinese blue and white porcelain teacups recovered from a sunken ship.

26

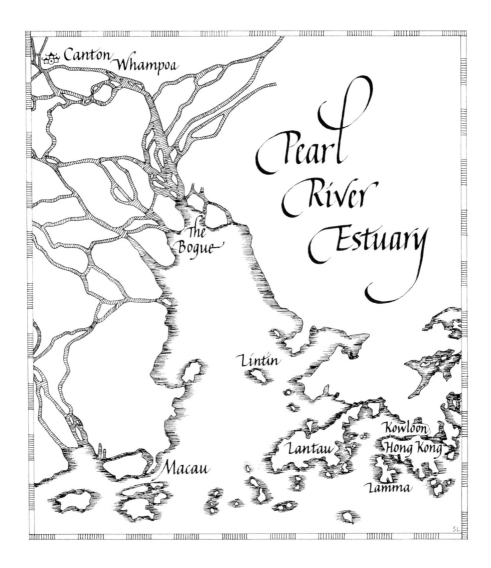

masse, as can be seen from the records of the Dutch East India Company and from the enormous cargoes that have been salvaged in recent decades from sunken ships. Such blue and white vases, dishes, drug jars and ewers were to influence Dutch Delftware in the seventeenth century and ultimately the Scottish potteries in the mid-eighteenth century.

The west was not slow to see the potential of the Chinese porcelain factories. European merchants and families began to place orders for sets of porcelain that could be used at home. James Drummond's blue and white Chinese dinner service includes all

the basic tableware as well as perforated fruit baskets, oval soup tureens and warming dishes. These were all shapes foreign to the Chinese potter. The Munro family of Foulis Castle in Ross-shire must have sent out to China a drawing or engraving of their castle, as well as a painting of their coat of arms, so that these could be copied on to porcelain in a Chinese factory near Canton. An engraving such as that of the Scottish piper by Francis Grose would have served as a pattern for the Chinese painter of the Scotsmen plate (see cover). The Chinese proved in general very adept at copying, although mistakes did occur: on one or two plates in the Brodie family service at Brodie Castle in Morayshire the word UNITE has been mispainted as UNTIE.

Much of this export porcelain would have been ordered through the British East India Company, but the Scots also had strong links with the Swedish East India Company, founded in 1731 and based in Gothenburg. Just as there

The kind of Chinese blue and white porcelain that appealed to Portuguese and Dutch traders in the sixteenth century.

Plate made in China for the Munro family of Foulis Castle in Ross-shire. Note the castle, the coat of arms, the crest and the two port scenes, perhaps one in China and the other in England.

Opposite: James Drummond's dinner service of Chinese blue and white porcelain, made about 1800.

This engraving by Francis Grose of 1797 is a copy of one by George Bickham, which served as a model for the Chinese painter of the Scotsmen plate (see cover).

Tea drinking in Scotland in 1817: this detail from David Wilkie's The Breakfast *shows how well established tea drinking had become by this date. Note also the Chinese vase on the mantelpiece.*

were Scottish traders in the Netherlands, so too were there a number in Sweden, some of them serving as supercargoes with the Swedish East India Company. Among these were Charles Irvine and Colin Campbell through whom a great many Scots placed their orders for Chinese porcelain (and also, presumably, for rhubarb root, as Irvine and Campbell made speculative imports of this too).

The tea table was probably the strongest stimulant to the import of Chinese porcelain as the vogue for tea drinking caught on and necessitated equipment. Lady Grisell Baillie's tea table at Mellerstain would have been one of the earliest in Scotland, and by the mid-eighteenth century tea tables would have sported not only a teapot (either of metal or porcelain), but also cups with handles as the enthusiasm for Chinese handleless cups waned, a milk jug and sugar basin, a slop bowl, a flat dish for teaspoons and a container for the tea leaves. Tea containers became known as caddies, because the early orders for tea from Chusan and Amoy were made up in small porcelain jars containing between one and four 'catties' of tea, a catty weighing just over a pound. (This is another linguistic indication that the British had succeeded in exporting tea from their early bases at Chusan and Amoy in the 1670s.) Porcelain caddies were later put on little three-legged stands known as teapoy, this term being used eventually to denote the caddy itself. By the late eighteenth century locking wooden tea boxes were considered the most practical, many of them incorporating two or three lidded containers for different types or grades of tea, and a glass mixing bowl.

What is so fascinating is that British trade with China in the eighteenth century caused a mini domestic revolution in Britain. Tea replaced beer and ale as the everyday drink, and

Two Chinese blue and white porcelain teapots, made for export in the 18th century.

Chinese porcelain tea caddy, handled cup and dish for holding teaspoons, made for export in the 18th century.

Chinese porcelain milk jug, made for export in the 18th century.

Chinese porcelain covered sugar bowl and Chinese-style handleless cup in a deep saucer, made for export in the 18th century.

porcelain, or China-ware as it was known, replaced wooden and pewter tableware. The steady rise in the consumption of tea however was matched by a decline in the import of Chinese porcelain. By the end of the eighteenth century Europe's own porcelain industry was developed to the point where it could match the quality and cost of Chinese export ware.

Indeed this revolution might even be called the breakfast revolution. Tea and porcelain found their way on to the breakfast table along with toast, and even the toast was transformed by the China trade. Long before the Portuguese brought sweet oranges and the miniature, slightly bitter kumquats to Europe from China in the sixteenth century, the bitter orange which we know today as the Seville or marmalade orange had found its way from China to Europe, perhaps along the Silk Route. Inspired by the Portuguese habit of making a preserve from quinces, known as *marmelada*, the British began in the seventeenth century to make a similar thick preserve from bitter oranges. It

Chinese porcelain teapoy or tea caddy, made for export in the 18th century.

Locking wooden tea caddy with compartments for both black and green tea, and a glass mixing bowl, sometimes used for sugar. Probably made in Scotland in the late 18th or early 19th century.

was no doubt considered beneficial first thing in the morning as the rind has tonic qualities which stimulate the appetite.

The breakfast revolution was of course lamented by some. In 1729 William Mackintosh of Borlum in Inverness-shire was to write in his agricultural treatise: 'When I came to my friend's house of a morning, I used to be asked if I had my morning draught yet? I am now asked if I have had my tea? And in lieu of the big quaigh with strong ale and toast, and after a dram of good wholesome Scots spirits, there is now the tea-kettle put to the fire, the tea-table and silver and china equippage brought in, and marmalade and cream'. Dr Samuel Johnson, on the other hand, who travelled through Scotland in 1773, was of the opinion that breakfast was 'a meal in which the Scots must be confessed to excel us'. This was because he enjoyed the tea, the coffee and the marmalade.

Tea and porcelain were of course not the sole exports carried by the East Indiamen. Medicinal drugs such as rhubarb root and China root made up a portion of the cargo, as did silk and cotton. Most of the silk exported from China was in the form of raw silk thread, either the fine white silk thread from Nanjing, or the coarser silk thread from Canton. If any of this silk found its way to Scotland it would have come indirectly via the Netherlands or England. We know that the shipments made by Andrew Russell, Scottish factor for trade in Rotterdam in the second half of the seventeenth century, contained the occasional 'small matted bundell silk stuffs' bound for Leith, and that in the first few years of the eighteenth century Lady Baillie was buying silk slippers and lengths of silk for window curtains and aprons. Lady Baillie's silk may have come from England, as by 1700 almost half of the textile imports to Scotland from England were silks, many of them made by the Spitalfield weavers in London, but some imported from the east and perhaps China. It is possible that some of the Chinese silk thread imported by the East India Company found its way to Paisley, near Glasgow, where the weaving of silk gauze became big business from 1759 until the 1780s.

Evidence for the sale or use in Scotland of Chinese cotton is scant. The most popular form of cotton from China was a finely woven, shiny, naturally yellow fabric from Nanjing, known as nankeen, some of which was made into trousers that acquired the

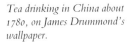
Tea drinking in China about 1780, on James Drummond's wallpaper.

34

name nankins. Nankeen does appear, along with complete tea and coffee services, in advertisements for the sale of cargo from China in the *Aberdeen Journal* in 1776 and 1778. It is hard to imagine that certain Scots would not at least have shown some interest in any available Chinese silk or cotton, as textile weaving was such a strong tradition in Scotland.

Just as silk and nankeen were being imported from China, textiles formed a small part of the British cargoes bound for China from London. The East India Company traders tried to interest the Chinese in British textiles and woollen fabrics, perhaps some of the latter from Scotland. Scottish trade with England had opened up enormously after the union of the Scottish and English parliaments of 1707, when many Scottish packmen began to carry textiles and woollens to England. It is not inconceivable that some of these found their way on to ships bound for China. The Chinese, however, were not keen on woollen textiles: they preferred their traditional padded silk and cotton garments.

What, therefore, did the Chinese want from trade with the British and other western countries? The answer, sadly, is not much. The incoming cargoes of the sixteen East Indiamen to call at Canton in 1792 comprised, from England, woollens, lead and tin, and, from India, cotton, pepper and sandalwood. By the time the lead and tin are partly discounted as serving mainly as ballast to stiffen the cargo of soft fabrics, these imports to China do not account for much.

Reluctance to accept foreign goods was the hallmark of China's attitude to trade with the west. The Chinese were interested in little other than silver, which they took in the form of Spanish dollars or 'pieces of eight', and sycee silver (from the Cantonese words for fine silk

Panel of silk, thought to be of Chinese origin, that was made into a dress in the mid-18th century.

on account of the fact that pure silver can be drawn out into fine threads). By the 1790s the restrictions imposed on foreign traders and the Chinese disinterest in western goods came to a head. The Qianlong emperor, whose reign from 1736 to 1796 ran concurrently with the East India Company's monopoly of the China trade, may have been one of China's greatest empire builders and constructor of extravagant Italian-style buildings and fountains, but in 1793 his letter to George III was to include the statement: 'We have never valued ingenious articles, nor do we have the slightest need of your country's manufactures'.

This letter was probably intended to deter the proposed visit to China by a British embassy led by Lord Macartney. The visit, which took place from 1793 to 1794, was the first of three attempts by the British to improve relations with China. Britain wanted to lift some of the trading restrictions, to try and get a permanent British representative in Beijing, and to secure the cession of a piece of land or an island such as Chusan near the principal tea and silk producing areas of China. All three missions failed. In fact all were probably doomed to fail from the start because neither country was willing or able to understand the other. One of the greatest barriers was of course language. Another was etiquette. To the Chinese, a nation so proud of its ancient civilization and apparently disinterested in and suspicious of what the west had to offer, the forceful British who had travelled so far to trade with them seemed barbaric and soon earned the names *hongmouren* or red-haired people, and *fanguai* or foreign devils. The Chinese expected all foreign visitors to come as kowtowing tribute bearers, not as envoys with ambassadors keen to negotiate.

The Macartney embassy of ninety-five men encompassed a military escort, a painter, an interpreter, a botanist whose name, David Stronach, would suggest he was of Scottish origin, a Scottish scientific experimenter, and, as might be expected, a Scottish physician, Dr Hugh Gillan from Morayshire. One cannot help wondering how many more Scots they would have encountered during their stay at the British factory in Macau, and we know that at least Macartney himself was at the receiving end of Scottish hospitality, from the very James Drummond whom we met earlier. In his fascinating journal Macartney relates: 'My quarters are at a house in the upper part of the town, rented by Mr Drummond who has been so good as to lend it me during his absence. It is most

Chinese sycee silver. The long curved pieces were known as shoes because of their resemblance to the shape of footwear worn by Chinese women with bound feet.

James Drummond's garden in Macau contained rocks associated with the Portuguese poet Luis de Camões who was exiled from Portugal in the 16th century. They were a favourite subject for artists such W G Tilesius von Tilenau whose engraving is entitled The Camoens Grotto in the Garden of Mr Drummond.

delightfully situated, and has a very pleasant romantic garden adjoining to it of considerable extent.'

It was to this house, now the municipal museum in Macau, that James Drummond would have retreated in the summer months. When Macartney stayed there in January 1794 just before his departure for home, Drummond was probably in Canton, overseeing East India Company business at the height of the trading season. By the time James Drummond was ready to retire to Scotland eighteen years later, in 1812, the East India Company's heyday was nearing its end. Its success had been mainly due to two factors: its well built ships and its dedicated high-quality staff.

One of the attractions to East India Company employees was in fact what was eventually to play a large part in the company's downfall: the lure of so-called privilege tonnage. With a little space of his own in a ship, a company employee could indulge in a little speculative buying on his private account, which could prove profitable if the goods of his choice sold well at home. One Scot who was to take full advantage of his privilege tonnage, and who was prepared to stop at nothing, was William Jardine. And his involvement brings us to the third important medicinal drug in the story: opium.

3
Free trade begins

Like many of his Scottish forebears employed by the East India Company, William Jardine, from Lochmaben in Dumfriesshire, had a diploma in medicine from the Royal College of Surgeons in Edinburgh. In 1802, at the age of eighteen, he joined an East India Company ship as surgeon's mate. Promotion on subsequent voyages allowed him privilege space in which to ship a little cargo on his own account from China to India and back. On the discovery that his private trading led to better returns than his salary as a ship's surgeon, he left the East India Company and, using the capital he had amassed from his private trade, formed a partnership to operate a new ship, the *Sarah*, between Bombay and Canton.

As far as the East India Company was concerned trading by private merchants was acceptable on the route between India and China, and the company granted licences to private merchants to trade in Canton. In the year 1792 there were sixteen Company ships in Canton and twenty-three private ships. From the 1770s these 'country traders' as they were known shipped Indian cotton and opium to China, and raw silk from China back to India. The East India Company had a monopoly on all the opium grown in Bengal, but in response to Chinese requests not to bring opium into the country and in order not to jeopardize the company's privileged trading position in Canton, it took the expedient alternative of auctioning off the opium in Calcutta to private traders rather than shipping it itself. These private traders shipped the opium to Lintin Island (p27), near Canton, where they sold it to Chinese smugglers in exchange for silver. This silver was subsequently sold by the private traders to the East India Company in Canton, in exchange for bills payable in London or India, and the East India Company used the silver to buy tea.

In a roundabout way then the private trade in opium helped to finance the traditional East India Company trade in tea. In other words, one drug supported another. The Chinese were less pleased however as their supply of silver was fast diminishing: more silver was being paid out for opium than was being received back as payment for tea.

William Jardine was not the only Scot speculating in the export of opium from India to China. By the early 1820s Jardine had met up in Canton with a fellow Scot, James Matheson from Lairg in Sutherland, who, while acting as an independent agent for firms engaged in the country trade with India, had also realized the potential for profit in the

Westerners negotiate better trading terms with Chinese officials, over the decanter of cherry brandy, off the island of Chusan in 1840 (detail). Failure to reach agreement led to the British bombardment and occupation of the island and the continuation of the Anglo-Chinese war.

William Jardine, often known as the Iron-headed Old Rat because his head had on one occasion appeared impervious to the beatings of an angry Chinese.

James Matheson, the younger partner of William Jardine.

opium trade. In 1832 the two men were to set up in partnership, thereby establishing the company known as Jardine, Matheson and Company that dominated the China trade and many other aspects of business in the east until fairly recently.

This great trading house was therefore founded under the auspices of the third medicinal drug in our story: opium. Following in the footsteps of rhubarb root which cured constipation, and tea which not only aided the digestion but also revived the mind and contributed to social intercourse, opium has suffered from a less good press.

Opium is produced from the juice of the unripe seed head of the poppy (*Papaver somniferum*), which is extracted and dried to make a brown gummy substance. Among many ancient civilizations this substance was consumed raw as a medicine: it acted both as a cure for dysentery and as a mild antidepressant. Such was the use of opium when it was introduced to China by the Turks and the Arabs in the eighth century. By the seventeenth century the Chinese were smoking it, sometimes mixed with tobacco, in their characteristic long thin-stemmed pipes. In this form it became a hallucinatory drug if consumed in large quantities. Smoked in moderation, however, it was probably no worse than moderate consumption of either alcohol or tobacco.

The problem was that overindulgence created addicts. A description of an opium addict is given by Robert Fortune, a Scottish plant collector whom we shall meet later: 'his looks were pale and haggard, his breathing quick and disturbed, and so thin was he, that his cheek bones seemed piercing the skin'. This man would have spent all his resources on opium, leaving him malnourished and in an extreme state of lethargy. We can perhaps understand therefore why the smoking of opium was officially banned in China in 1729. Fortune was also of the opinion, however, that 'the smuggling and the smoking of opium are very much exaggerated'. The East India Company had been warned that any ship importing opium would be confiscated. For this reason the trade in opium passed into the hands of private traders such as Jardine and Matheson and their rival English company Dent's.

In the years Jardine and Matheson were building up their individual businesses, opium was being imported freely into Britain where both raw opium and opium-based preparations were cheap and easily available from pharmacies. It was one of the most widely used drugs of the day, taken in pill form as a painkiller, similar to today's aspirin, or as a drink, known as laudanum, in which raw opium was mixed with distilled water and alcohol. Like rhubarb, opium was promoted by the Society of Arts which offered medals for its successful production. In fact the opium poppy-growing craze coincided exactly with the years of Jardine's and Matheson's trading success, and in 1830 an Edinburgh man received a gold medal for the quantities he had grown in the city.

It was only in the second half of the nineteenth century that there was a move to control the use of opium in Britain. Criticism was levelled at the overuse of opium as an antidepressant amongst factory workers, and at the soothing of fractious babies with poppy tea. To Jardine and Matheson therefore, whose main involvement with opium

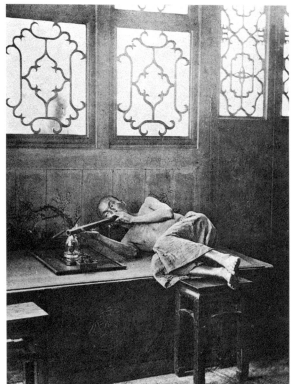

Opium smoker photographed by John Thomson in a restaurant in the 1870s.

Chinese opium smoking equipment. The opium was stored in the small cups to the right. The smoker would lift a drop of gummy opium with the spindle-shaped needle and heat it over the candle. When the opium bubbled, he would transfer it into the bowl of the pipe. He would then position the bowl of the pipe over the candle and inhale the resulting smoke. The process had to be repeated after every two or three puffs.

41

was before the days of widespread criticism in Britain, the promotion of opium in China probably seemed perfectly reasonable. In the words of a later Scottish missionary working in the interior of China, 'Opium smoking is on all fours with whisky drinking'. Moreover, at the time of writing, this missionary was able to witness what was going on inside China. In Jardine's and Matheson's time foreigners were not permitted to travel beyond the factory area of Canton and therefore could not see for themselves the extent of opium addiction.

Most important of all was the fact that the opium trade was extremely profitable. The British benefited: both the East India Company on whose estates in Bengal it was grown, and the private trader who sold it directly to the Chinese. And the Chinese too reaped profits: both those who smuggled the opium in from Lintin Island and the Cantonese officials who were perfectly happy to accept bribes from the private traders to turn a blind eye to the incoming drug.

Despite the official ban on opium smoking and on the import of the drug, Chinese officials appear to have had little intention of enforcing the ban. In Fortune's opinion, in the 1840s 'the Chinese government, whatever it may say, has no wish to put a stop to its introduction'. The Chinese would probably have preferred to ban western traders altogether and prevent the vast outflows of silver from their coffers. They may also have been keen to restrict the import of opium in order to protect their own growers. However, the most likely reason for the ineffectuality of the ban was probably that, as Fortune pointed out, 'The whole, or at least the greater part of the mandarins use it, and it is not at all unlikely that his Celestial Majesty himself makes one of the number of its devotees'. Fortune describes how, from time to time, Chinese war junks would approach the British opium vessels and beat gongs and fire guns at a distance. Completely oblivious to this by now familiar calamity, the opium vessels would wait until they were *requested* to leave their anchorage, which they would do, reluctantly, for a few days before returning to trade in the usual way. Thus the trade in opium continued, with a fairly stable four thousand chests a year being brought to Lintin by the private traders.

But if Jardine, Matheson and Co owed its beginnings to the opium trade, the company was soon to have the chance to diversify. In 1833, only one year after the founding of the company, the East India Company's monopoly of the China trade was ended due to pressure from British manufacturers. Private trading could now begin in earnest, and Jardine Matheson promptly led the way. In 1834 the *Sarah* was shipped out from Canton full of silks, nankeen cottons, knick-knacks, rhubarb root and China root.

Meanwhile back in Edinburgh another perspicacious Scot was quick to take advantage of the opening up of trade with China. This was Andrew Melrose. By 1834 Andrew Melrose was the leading tea dealer and grocer in Edinburgh, much of his success due to the fact that he tried wherever possible to buy his supplies from source. Tea of course he had been obliged to purchase at the auctions of the East India Company in London, but immediately following the end of its trading monopoly, Melrose was to seek the cooperation of Jardine Matheson in Canton. Melrose's request for six hundred packages of

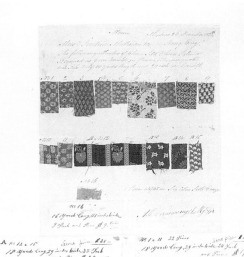

Painted silk shawls and valances like this one were the kind of silk piece good exported from China by Jardine Matheson and Co.

A page of orders for silk thread and tape from Jardine Matheson and Co.

43

tea was Jardine Matheson's first order for tea. On 28 November 1834 the tea was duly dispatched on the *Isabella* to Leith, where it aroused much excitement on its arrival almost six months later on 19 May 1835.

First Sale at Leith of Teas from China direct.— Yesterday being the first day that any teas, direct from China, had been offered for sale at the port of Leith, much interest was excited among those connected with the trade, and the attendance in the sale-room was numerous. There was considerable competition among the buyers, and the teas met a ready sale at prices as under, exclusive of duty :—Bohea, from 1s. 1½d. to 1s. 5d. per lb.; Congou, 1s. 4d. to 2s. 2½d. per do.; Grange pekoe, 2s. 6d. to 2s. 7¾d.; Capers, 1s. 1d. to 1s. 3d.; Blackleaf pekoe, 1s. 9d. to 2s. 0d.; Twankay, 1s. 9d. to 0s. 0d. Hyson, 2s. 9d. to 3s. 0d.; Gunpowder hyson, 2s. 9d. to 3s. 4d. The teas, upon the whole, were considered an excellent parcel. The same vessel (the Isabella) is, we understand, to go out for another cargo for the port of Leith, and may be expected home next March or April.

Leith Harbour would have looked much like this when Melrose's tea arrived from Canton on the Isabella in 1835. Note the juxtaposition of sail and steam. The engraving, dated 1829, from a drawing by Thomas Shepherd, makes an interesting comparison with the Canton waterfront on James Drummond's wallpaper (frontispiece).

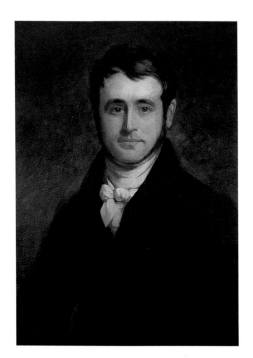

Andrew Melrose, Edinburgh's successful grocer and tea dealer who pioneered the direct shipment of tea from Canton to Leith.

The red packets that spell Melrose's to many Scots.

In anticipation of a rise in the tea business, Melrose had purchased new, larger premises in George Street in Edinburgh. The *Isabella's* teas may have excited the adult public, but of far greater import to a contemporary lad was the accompanying cargo of 'bamboo rattan canes which were counted a neccessary article for swelldom among us'.

Edinburgh's claim to have imported the first teas direct from China may however simply be a reflection of traditional Edinburgh-Glasgow rivalry. Reports in the *Glasgow Courier* of 1 November 1834 state that William Connal was at the receiving end of the first parcel of free-trade teas to Scotland. Intercity rivalry apart, credit must go to Andrew Melrose for continuing to promote the direct import of tea, and for getting even closer to the source after China opened up more fully in 1842.

But what led to the greater opening up of China and the founding of Hong Kong in 1842? In order to maintain a degree of control over British trade in Canton, the British government decided to send out a superintendent of trade who might also try to nego-tiate better trading terms with the Chinese. The first of these superintendents, Lord Napier of Merchiston, a Scot, failed, and died of fever shortly afterwards. He was replaced by Captain Charles Elliot who had to contend with the zealous Lin Zexu who had been sent simultaneously to Canton by the emperor to suppress the growing opium trade. This Lin attempted to do by seizing vast quantities and burning it, much to the anger of the British who immediately sought compensation. The petty scuffles that followed gave rise to another serious issue: that of whether a British man in China should

be subject to Chinese or British jurisdiction. However, the root cause of the first Anglo-Chinese war, often called the Opium War, was not opium but trade, the great British desire to lift the restrictions on trade with China. With her superior naval prowess Britain was victorious and forced China to sign the Treaty of Nanjing in 1842. This treaty gave the British a great deal of what they wanted: financial compensation for the opium that had been destroyed, the opening of five treaty ports along the China coast, namely, from south to north: Canton, Amoy, Fuzhou, Ningbo and Shanghai, and the cession of an island where they could live and trade under their own legislature. Chusan, the island near Shanghai where the British had had a base for some years, might have seemed the logical island in its proximity to the mouth of the Yangzi River which leads so deep into the interior of China. But when Captain Elliot and the British traders were

Hong Kong's mountains and coastal waters made many Scots feel quite at home.

forced out of Canton they retreated to their ships anchored in what appeared to be 'a solitary lake, lying in the bosom of a Highland glen'. This was the harbour of Hong Kong. And in his urgency to secure a firm trading base, Captain Elliot, in defiance of Lord Palmerston's lack of enthusiasm for an island he had never set eyes on, settled for the island of Hong Kong. The British flag was hoisted on 26 January 1841 and the British possession of Hong Kong became official in June 1843. In the treaty there was not a single mention of opium.

4
China opens up

News of the Treaty of Nanjing and the opening up of more Chinese ports reached Britain in November 1842, a month after the arrival in Canton of a young Scot of twenty-five: this was William Melrose, son of the Edinburgh grocer Andrew Melrose. Although William was not employed by his father at this stage, Andrew Melrose no doubt harboured hopes that his son's experience in tea-tasting would later prove useful to the family business. Once again the Melroses were taking instant advantage of the opening up of China to trade.

Sure enough, by 1848 William was working as sole tea-taster, or 'smellum' as the Chinese called them, for his father and Scottish business associates. The venture was a success. After five years the profits of Andrew Melrose had risen considerably and William himself had done well. William worked extremely hard, some-times 'tasting and comparing until I was almost sick and my mouth sore'.

Three factors contributed to the success of the Melrose family business. William chose his ships with great care at the dawn of an era in which the great ships raced to deliver the new season's teas from China to Britain in the shortest possible time. He was also meticulous about the often complex financial arrange-ments for his trading. But above all William's success was due to the constant stream of lengthy letters he sent to his father and business associates in Scotland, closely detailing the tea trade in China. These were the equivalent of today's phonecalls, faxes and e-mail, yet the post often took two months. But it was the

Chinese watercolours of insects and flowers were popular souvenirs brought or sent home by westerners working in Canton.

Reverse painting on glass (the crack shows clearly how the painting is on the glass rather than behind it). This type of painting, which became much more readily available with the opening up of China, was done specifically for export to the west, on glass imported from Europe.

communication that was so vital, as it kept both ends of the business abreast of what was going on.

These letters have survived and are important in another respect: they give us a lively insight into the day-to-day life of a Scottish expatriate in Canton and Macau, and show his remoteness from the political upheavals of the day. To imagine where William

One of William Melrose's shortest letters to his father, indicating how busy he was.

lived in Canton we have to look back at James Drummond's wallpaper (frontispiece). Although by William's time the British factory building on the wallpaper had been replaced by a more modern building, it was here, in a 'close, shut-in house' that William began life in Canton before confidence in his tea profits prompted him to move to a former *hong* merchant's house 'done up in English style' with two bedrooms, office, tea room and dining room, all carpeted with 'red-flowered' matting and with a verandah overlooking the waterfront. When business was calm, William would retreat to the laid-back, decaying Portuguese elegance of Macau, in whose cool sea breezes he would relax by riding, hunting and shooting, some-times sharing his picnic of cold beef, bread and brandy with 'civil and social' Chinamen. He liked a 'look of the *Scotsman* once a month' and even took up drawing under the tutelage of the elderly George Chinnery, the prolific Macau-based artist and eccentric socialite. It was Chinnery who claimed that the average British trader spent 'six months in Macau, having

William Melrose drawn by Thomas Boswall Watson.

The area occupied by the Canton factories can be seen very clearly in this drawing done after the fire of 1856 by Walter George Dickson, Scottish sketching companion of Thomas Boswall Watson.

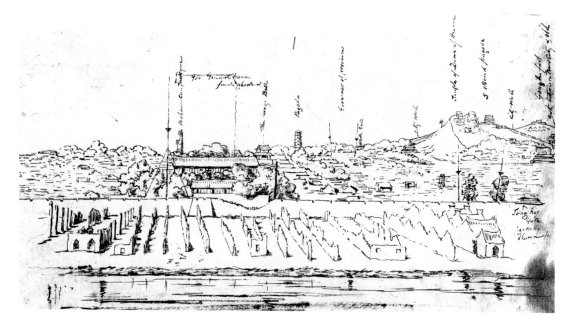

nothing to do, and the other six months in Canton, doing nothing'. William Melrose was one exception.

None of William's sketches seem to have survived. However a great number of those of Chinnery's Edinburgh-born doctor, Dr Thomas Boswall Watson, have, including a small portrait of William. William often stayed with the Watsons in Macau, where Dr Watson must have looked forward to William's company as he suffered from isolation (there were only three other British families), from a surfeit of Portuguese patients whose ailments he had to diagnose in faltering Portuguese, and from personal ill health. William too felt 'quite at home with them' and sad to leave Macau at the end of February after his Christmas break: 'Leaving this place to go up to Canton puts me in mind of leaving Pendreich to go into Edinburgh after a month's holiday'.

But the tea trade was pressing. By April the new season's tea shoots would be gathered and prepared, and William would be urgently selecting the best teas, always paying heed to his father's comments on which types were selling well at home in Scotland. The advertisement from an Edinburgh newspaper of 1835 for the tea shipped by the *Isabella* shows types and quantities similar to those shipped by William:

> ## TEAS.
> To be Sold by auction, in the Exchange Sale-room, Leith, on Tuesday, 19th inst. at 10 o'clock,
>
> 4318 PACKAGES CONGO — —
>
> | | | |
> |---|---|---|
> | 2103 | // | Bohea |
> | 860 | // | Pekoe |
> | 189 | // | Twankay |
> | 220 | // | Caper |
> | 174 | // | Hyson |
> | 80 | // | Gunpowder |
> | 25 | // | Ankoi |
> | 10 | // | Campoi |
> | 10 | // | Imperial |
>
> 8000
>
> Being the entire cargo of the ship Isabella, James Robertson, commander, direct from Canton. The teas are landing in fine order, and are pronounced to be very superior in quality. Mr Hulbert, from London, is to inspect and character the whole; and the teas will be on shew in the warehouse three days previous to the sale.
>
> For further information apply, in London, to
> Messrs HULBERT, LAYTON, & CO.;
> or here, to
> JAMES DUNCAN & CO.
> Leith, 7th May 1835.

A tea-taster's life and work in China, *from* The Illustrated London News, *13 October 1888. The accompanying article says that tea 'contributes more to the household comfort of English families than all other foreign commodities, except wheat and flesh-meat' and 'is first in importance among Chinese exports to Great Britain'.*

AT THE OFFICE.

CARRYING TEA-CHESTS TO THE SHIP.

TEA IN BED.

TASTING TEA.

WEIGHING TEA-CHESTS.

ON BOARD SHIP.

A TEA-TASTER'S LIFE AND WORK IN CHINA.

Green teas on the left: the best Chinese Dragon's Well tea that was not exported, Hyson Pekoe with its white silky down, and Gunpowder or Caper with its tightly curled leaves. Black teas on the right: the smaller orange-tipped leaves would approximate to Orange Pekoe, the larger wiry ones to Congo or Bohea.

Bills of lading for William Melrose's over-enthusiastic shipment of green teas and for his knick-knacks.

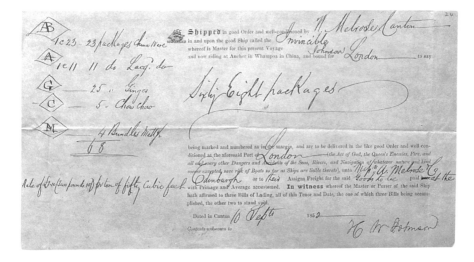

The cases of black tea – Congo (meaning hard work), Bohea (from the mountains of that name) and Pekoe (the name describing the white silky down on the early leaf buds) – far outnumber the green Twankay, Caper (so called from its resemblance to green caper buds), Hyson (meaning sunny springtime) and Gunpowder, suggesting that tastes had changed little over the century since Lady Grisell Baillie's orders for tea. The price however had dropped considerably, fine teas costing only four shillings (twenty pence) a pound and common teas only two shillings (ten pence). William shows his sound business judgement in his determination to ship teas direct to Leith or Glasgow because 'the kinds that please the Leith people may be had much cheaper here . . . than those that please the London people'. We see hints of disagreement too between father and son: William's preference for 'tarry' teas is not shared by his father, and an enthusiastic shipment by William of Gunpowder green tea sold so poorly that Andrew nicknamed it the Gunpowder Plot, for which William apologized 'You are rather hard on me about . . . the gunpowder; however, I won't blow up about it'.

Far harder in William's opinion than the purchase of teas was 'buying curiosities', for which William foresaw a potential market back home. The kinds of knick-knacks William picked up cheaply are listed in this advertisement from the *Edinburgh Evening Courant* of December 1850:

CHINA GOODS.

To be SOLD, without reserve, on Wednesday and Thursday, 18th and 19th curt., at No. 10 EXCHANGE BUILDINGS, LIVERPOOL, by T. & H. LITTLEDALE & CO.,

THE Entire Shipment of CHINA GOODS ex the Ship "Duilius," consisting of 350 Packages of Vases and other China Wares, Ginger, Cabinets, Tables, Writing Desks, Mandarin and Ladies' Dresses, Tortoiseshell Combs, China Ink, Chessmen, Ivory Balls, Glass Paintings, Grass Cloth, Handkerchiefs, Lamps, Gongs, Images, Birds, Insects, Folding Screens, and a great variety of other valuable articles.

Apply to

T. & H. LITTLEDALE & CO.,
Liverpool ; or
ANDREW MELROSE & CO.,
Edinburgh.

These are the very items which have become synonymous with the China trade of the mid-nineteenth century but which were really little more than an adjunct to the tea trade. Tea, however, was not only responsible for Chinese knick-knacks. Of far wider-reaching significance was the impact of tea on Scotland's shipbuilding industry.

The advent of competitive free trade on the abolition in 1833 of the East India Company's monopoly meant that speed became a matter of vital importance. As a result, the relatively slow East Indiamen gradually gave way to smaller, faster ships which could complete the voyage from China to Britain in three to four months rather than six to nine. Although steamships were being constructed by this time, their use as cargo ships had not been perfected: their huge fuel consumption meant that the hold was occupied by coal bunkers not cargo, their cargoes being predominantly people mail, and small valuable goods. The ever-increasing quantities of tea being exported from China continued to be carried in tightly packed square-rigged sailing ships, which by the 1850s had become known as tea clippers. These were perfected in Aberdeen in the early 1850s by firms such as Alexander Hall, Walter Hood and John Duthie. Aberdeen orders were boosted and Clyde shipbuilders such as Robert Steele and Charles Connell were encouraged to compete in the building of even faster, more capacious, ships. The Clyde took the lead in the 1860s. Every year throughout the 1850s and 1860s these tea clippers competed in the race to bring home China's new season teas, the ships often arriving within hours of each other over a journey of three or four months.

In 1869 the Clyde produced one of the world's fastest ships, the *Cutty Sark*. Nothing gives a better idea of just how closely packed with tea such clippers were, and the cramped

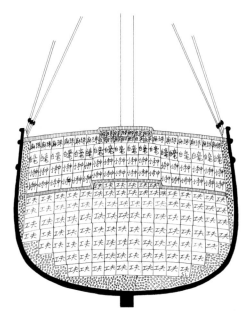

Tea clippers were absolutely jammed with tea chests, the more expensive teas being placed above the cheaper ones.

Chinese fan of ivory and goose feathers, with its black and gold lacquer box, 19th century.

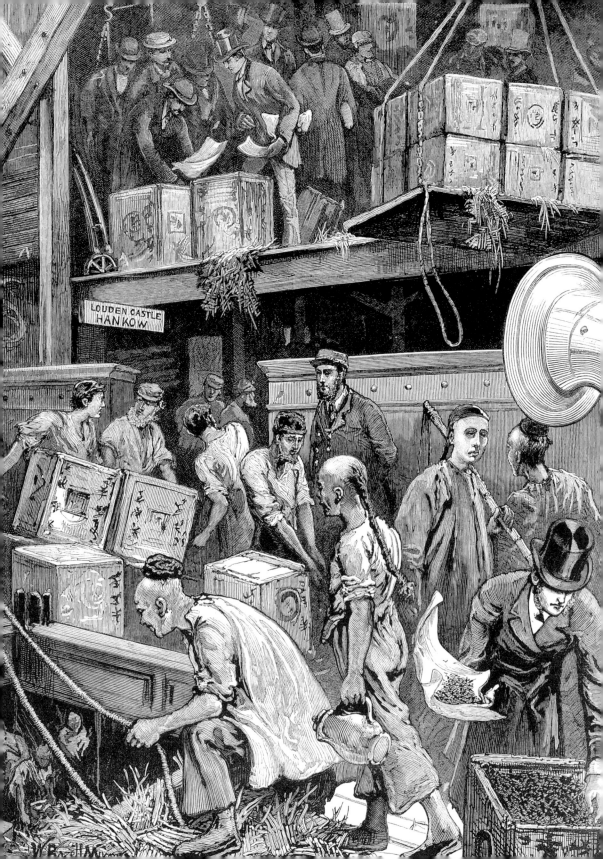

LOUDEN CASTLE
HANKOW

The Cutty Sark *by J E Cooper.*

and uncomfortable conditions of life on board, than a visit to the *Cutty Sark* preserved in dry dock today at Greenwich. The ship's officers may have had individual cabins and a wood-panelled saloon with a fireplace, but the twenty or so crew members slept eight to a deckhouse, the lower bunks frequently soaked by seawater. Daily rations consisted of seven pints of water each, three of which had to be given up to soak the salted meat or lentils that provided the mainstay of the diet, padded out with ship's biscuits and the odd chicken from the coops on deck on special occasions.

It is ironic that the very year the *Cutty Sark* was launched also heralded the demise of the tea clipper. The opening of the Suez Canal in 1869 halved the length of journeys to the east by steamship and caused the ultimate eclipse of sail by steam. And by this time the Clyde had established itself as the world's leading shipbuilding river: in 1871 Clyde shipyards produced forty-five steamships for use in the China trade. Tea had therefore not only stimulated Clyde shipbuilding but had prolonged the building of sailing ships.

It was on a steam passenger ship that William Melrose had made his two-month outward journey to China in 1848. Having left Southampton on the *Ripon*, he sailed via

Tea being unloaded from a clipper, from The Illustrated London News, *8 December 1877. This particular ship, the* Louden Castle, *contained 40,000 packages of tea, amounting to 2 million pounds in weight.*

59

Gibraltar and Malta to Alexandria, where he picked up the mail from China. He then travelled up the Nile to Cairo, crossing the desert from there by road to Suez, and joining the *Bentinck* for Ceylon (now Sri Lanka). There he boarded the *Braganza,* on which he crossed paths with another Scot also bound for a tea-related mission in China. This was Robert Fortune from Kelloe in Berwickshire. That these two Scots appear not to have become acquainted on board sums up one aspect of the tea trade. Here was William Melrose with a profound knowledge of tea leaves and the drink, yet, as with his forebears in the tea trade, no apparent curiosity about the origins of the plant. And here was a fellow Scot dispatched to China for that very purpose: to seek out this enigmatic plant which China's barriers had kept hidden all those centuries.

This was Robert Fortune's second trip to China. Sent as a botanical collector for the Horticultural Society in London as soon as news of peace with China reached Britain in the autumn of 1842, Fortune was to take much greater advantage of the freedom to travel in China's interior than William Melrose ever did. Unlike previous Scots with an interest in foreign plants such as rhubarb, Fortune was not a medical man. Two years' apprenticeship at the Royal Botanic Garden in Edinburgh followed by a year as super-intendent of the Horticultural Society's hothouses in Chiswick had given him a sound knowledge of plants. He knew nothing however about plant collecting or foreign travel, but was soon to prove himself more than capable of the job. A fearless traveller in his disguise as a Chinese man with shaved head, wig and pigtail, he was on one occasion chased and stoned by robbers, and on another managed to fend off pirates in the South China Sea while in the throes of a fever. All this he was to record most conscientiously in three volumes about his 'wanderings'.

Fortune had been inspired to seek out this ' "flowery land", the land of camellias, azaleas, and roses, of which I had heard so much in England' through the enthusiasm of John Reeves, a former tea-taster with the East India Company in Canton and then chairman of the Horticultural Society's Chinese committee. Reeves had brought back with him five volumes of exquisite watercolours of Chinese plants, fruits and vegetables, painted by Chinese artists. Almost photographic in their precision, such watercolours provided evidence for the likes of Fortune of what could be found in China. These were not the first such botanical paintings to reach Britain. More than a century earlier, about 1700, a set of more roughly executed paintings of Chinese plants had been sent by James Cuninghame, a Scottish surgeon with the East India Company, from Amoy to the botanist James Petiver in London. Cuninghame had also sent home from both Amoy and Chusan several hundred dried plant specimens, including the first camellia to be seen in Europe.

In Cuninghame's time the transport of live plants was a problem. The sea voyage was long and wet, and if there was shortage of fresh water or space on board, plants would have been one of the first items to meet their end overboard. Fortune, however, was to benefit from a breakthrough in plant transportation: Nathaniel Ward's glazed cases. In fact Fortune was one of the pioneers of the use of these miniature portable greenhouses, extolling their praise in a letter to Ward: 'We have done wonders with your cases . . . When I tell you that nearly twenty thousand tea-plants were taken in *safety* and in *high health* from Shanghae [sic] to the Himalayas, you will have an idea of our success'. And success it was! Although Fortune cannot accept full credit for seeking out the tea plant in China and introducing it to India, he certainly played a large part in the story. How little aware he would have been of the consequences of his success: by the late 1860s Assam tea was being consumed in Britain and by the 1880s tea was being shipped from Ceylon. The British preference for Indian teas eventually brought about the decline of the China tea trade and today China teas constitute only a very small portion of the market.

Fortune's searches in the tea-producing districts of Fujian province had another important consequence. He managed to establish and make public the fact that both green and black teas originated from the one species of plant, the *Camellia sinensis,* of which he noted varieties. The fact that Fortune is always given credit for this must be the result of the wide distribution of his writings. It seems to have gone unnoticed that John Bell in his *Travels* of 1763 observed that 'Both the green and bohea [black tea] grow on the same tree, or rather shrub, called by the CHINESE tzay'. Fortune could expand on the subject however because he was able to watch how the tea leaves were processed, and explain the difference between unfermented green teas and fermented black teas.

Chinese watercolours such as this one of the Azalea indica, *brought back from Canton by John Reeves, would have inspired plant collectors like Robert Fortune to go in search of such flowers.*

Ward's case: this mini portable greenhouse was developed by Nathaniel Ward for the transport of live plants from overseas.

Processing tea: picking, firing, transporting the chests, decorating the chests.

Fortune describes how the topmost leaves of the tea plant are picked in April and May, into round baskets. They then have to be dried, yet not so much as to lose their flavour. All the leaves are first tossed about with a bamboo brush in a large drying pan for about five minutes to make them pliable. They are then thrown on to a table, where each worker gathers together a bundle which he moulds like bread dough to twist and condense the leaves. After this the leaves are exposed to the open air for a time, longer if they are to be made into black tea as exposure encourages fermentation. The final process creates the colour and taste distinction between green and black teas: the teas that are to remain green are dried in a sieve over a slow fire for about an hour, whereas those leaves destined to become black teas are tossed in a pan over a charcoal fire until they turn black. The leaves are then sorted according to quality and loaded into boxes for transport.

By disseminating this knowledge to 'the man of science and the merchant' Fortune made a valuable contribution to our understanding of tea, although the majority of us probably drink our daily tea in almost the same ignorance of its origins and processing as the earliest tea drinkers. Fortune's contributions to the British garden are undoubtedly better appreciated. In his travels from Hong Kong to the newly opened ports and then inland to the tea districts, Fortune collected a number of plants that few of us probably associate now with China: azaleas (some of which we now call rhododendrons), camellias, roses and peonies. Even before retiring to Scotland in the 1860s he was able to comment that a number of his introductions 'are now growing in our gardens in England'.

Like William Melrose, Fortune also collected Chinese knick-knacks, which he sold back home. Sadly, in all his writings Fortune never mentions his personal circumstances or his family, although he is said to have spent part of each of his eighteen years' retirement in Scotland on his son's farm in East Lothian.

A western merchant comes to buy tea. The tea is being tramped into chests before being weighed.
Page from an album of watercolours painted by a Chinese artist for export to the west about 1800.

The Chinese were well accustomed to transporting live plants by water.

More intrepid than Fortune in his plant collecting excursions in China, and almost unethical in the prolificacy of his collections, was George Forrest who was born in Falkirk in Stirlingshire in 1873. Forrest's interest in botany developed during his training as a pharmacist in Kilmarnock in Ayrshire, and subsequently in the herbarium at the Royal Botanic Garden in Edinburgh. It was here that he was singled out by the regius keeper Sir Isaac Bayley Balfour as a suitable candidate to undertake a plant collecting expedition to China for a wealthy Liverpool cotton broker who wanted to establish a garden of rare and new plants.

In 1904 Forrest set out for southwest China, to the province of Yunnan, which had been little explored by foreigners. Due to its climate, southwest China is rich in temperate and alpine flora, such as rhododendrons, primulas and gentians, with which Forrest is particularly identified. He was always encouraged by Bayley Balfour, to whom he sent many of his species for identification.

Unlike Fortune, Forrest was not a writer. He was, however, a photographer, and his seven expeditions to southwest China between 1904 and 1932 are extensively documented by his as yet unpublished collection of black and white photographs. Despite an early unfortunate incident in 1905, when some Tibetans attacked the French mission where Forrest and his seventeen men were staying, killing sixty-six of the eighty inhabitants, Forrest was not put off by China. He took the trouble to learn Chinese and trained local collectors to assist him in his exploratory searches. These resulted in the collection of over 30,000 species, over 5000 of them rhododendrons, and many of them still popular today. In fact Forrest can be said to have transformed a great number of our rock gardens and woodland parks with his introductions, which flourish particularly well in the temperate climate of the west of Scotland.

The Primula forrestii, *named after George Forrest who collected numerous varieties of primula in southwest China.*

George Forrest disguised in Chinese dress after his escape from Tibetan marauders.

Forrest's ability to communicate and work with the local Chinese must have endeared him to the missionaries with whom he set up base in southwest China. In fact he benefited enormously from his association with them. They, like him, were taking advantage of the opening up of the interior of China. The French were by no means the only missionaries tilling the Chinese field: among the most adventurous of all the missionaries were the Scots whose strong grasp of the reforming powers of the church inspired them to spread Christianity as far afield as China. Perhaps the most remarkable contingent of Scottish missionaries was that which ventured as far north as Manchuria from the 1860s, and was to remain there until the 1950s.

In fact these Scottish Presbyterians were reintroducing Christianity to an area not so remote from its initial entry point. As early as the seventh century Nestorian missionaries had brought Christianity into northwestern China from Western Asia, and by the beginning of the seventeenth century Jesuit missionaries, who came to China on Portuguese ships, were permitted to reside in the Chinese court in Beijing because they were considered a useful source of western science. From 1717 until the beginning of the nineteenth century Christianity was frowned upon. The arrival in China in 1807 of Robert Morrison, born in Jedburgh in Roxburghshire, with the London Missionary Society set the pattern for an ever-increasing stream of foreign missionaries who, by 1845, were permitted to live and work in the five treaty ports, and after 1860 to travel much further into the interior of China.

Missionaries played only a lateral role in trade, some of them being employed by merchants for their knowledge of the Chinese language which made them useful as interpreters. Robert Morrison was in fact to translate the Bible into Chinese and to write a Chinese dictionary. More than anything else missionaries served as exporters and importers of knowledge, many of them returning eventually to the west to enhance our understanding of China and its language and culture. Two of their most important 'exports' were education and western medicine, which they promoted by setting up schools and hospitals. As we have seen, the Scots have always been particularly strong in the medical field, so it is not surprising to find that a large number of Scotland's missionaries were also doctors. One such was Dugald Christie from Glencoe in the Highlands, who was invited in 1882 by the United Presbyterian Church of Scotland to be their first medical missionary to Manchuria. That same year he arrived in Mukden (now Shenyang) in China's northern Liaoning province. Christie's aim was to establish a Chinese medical profession in Manchuria which would then serve the local Chinese. By raising his own funds and winning the support of the local Chinese through his successful anti-plague campaign in 1910, Christie was able to open the Mukden Medical College in 1912. By 1921 its hospital had 140 beds, twenty-four Chinese nurses administered by a British matron, six fully qualified Chinese surgeons and an outpatient department. Christie was held in such high esteem by the Chinese that he was presented with Chinese robes which he took great pride in wearing.

It was not unusual for missionaries who won the hearts of their converts to be given most valuable gifts. The jade *ruyi* (meaning 'as you wish' and serving as a token of well-

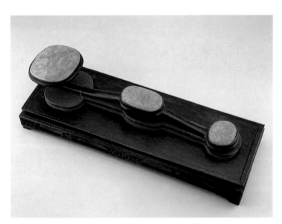

The jade ruyi *presented to Basil Livingstone Learmonth on his retirement.*

Basil Livingstone Learmonth leaves his Chinese colleagues at Yanjing University in Beijing in 1937.

wishing) presented to Dr Basil Livingstone Learmonth on his retirement from the post of medical officer at Yanjing University in Beijing in 1937, is a case in point. Items of jade were not made for export by the Chinese, partly because jade was considered too precious to the Chinese and partly because most westerners failed to appreciate its beauty. The Chinese have long considered jade as embodying the most noble of human virtues. In this sense an object of jade was the most fitting gift for a man such as Livingstone Learmonth who had devoted over forty years of his life to the Chinese people. After graduating in medicine from the University of Edinburgh, Learmonth travelled overland to Manchuria to work as a missionary in Xinmin, not far from Mukden. In 1915 he took up his post in Beijing, marrying another Scottish doctor who set up first a women's clinic in the city, then a rural community funded by the handicrafts made by the women. When we think back to the women on John Bell's embassy to China in 1720 who were turned back from the northern border, and then to the exclusion of all European women from Canton, here at last we have a western woman not only entering, but also working in China.

People such as Dugald Christie and the Livingstone Learmonths epitomize the tenacity and dedication of the Scottish missionaries in China. That the Protestant missionaries in Manchuria were one of the last groups to leave in the 1950s when they were no longer welcome under Communist rule is also indicative of their determination. The relative success of the medical care and the conversion to Christianity of a

Dugald Christie receives the Imperial Order of the Double Dragon in the form of robes, a decorative umbrella, and an official button, 1897.

那裏任意放蕩浪費貲財。既耗盡了一切所有的又遇着那地方大遭饑荒就窮苦起來。於是去投靠那地方的一個人那人打發他到田裏去放豬。他恨不得拿豬所喫的豆莢充飢也沒

huge number of Chinese was not what Robert Fortune foresaw in the 1840s. In his opinion the majority of Chinese were 'entirely indifferent to religion of any kind' and the remainder were 'so bigoted and conceited, that it will be a most difficult task to convince them that any religion is better or purer than their own'.

Fortune was never shy to express his opinion on China and the Chinese. In the decades following Fortune's visits to China, another Scot, from Edinburgh, was to set out with precisely this aim, to provide 'some insight into the present condition of the inhabitants of the vast Chinese empire'. This was John Thomson. What sets Thomson apart from previous Scottish commentators on China was the fact that he was first and foremost a photographer. Yet his magnificent series of two hundred photographs of China and its people, published in 1874, is accompanied by lengthy explanatory captions, making him one of the first true photojournalists. His subsequent *Ten Years' Travels, Adventures and Residence Abroad,* published in 1874, abounds in lively witty descriptions, many of which bear close comparison with the impressions of Robert Fortune.

Both Fortune and Thomson visited Shanghai, the northernmost of the five treaty ports to be opened up by the Treaty of Nanjing in 1842. Fortune foresaw that Shanghai would 'doubtless become one day a place of vast importance, in a commercial point of view' and Thomson commented that there was a 'splendour and sumptuousness about its buildings'. Fortune's prediction was spot on. Situated at the mouth of the Yangzi River, midway between north and south China, and close to the major tea, silk and cotton producing areas of China, Shanghai was ideally placed to blossom as a port. Boats of all sizes brought from the interior 'large quantities of tea and silk to supply the wants of our merchants', returning 'loaded with the manufactures of Europe and America', especially Britain's 'plain cotton goods'. From its early days as a port, Shanghai was to

John Thomson set out to photograph all aspects of Chinese life. He also sent Chinese curiosities to Edinburgh where they were sold at a profit for the Blind Asylum. He may have bought them from dealers such as these in Beijing.

Missionaries translated the Bible into Chinese and produced posters illustrating biblical stories, here the episode in the story of the Prodigal Son when the son in question embarks on his spendthrift excursions. Note the depiction of Chinese rather than Western protagonists.

flourish as a major industrial city, producing predominantly textiles. Westerners, partic-ularly Lancashire-trained cotton workers, helped set up cotton mills, and trade was carried on by branches of the large trading houses such as Jardine Matheson, Dent's and Russell's, whose employees lived a life of expatriate isolation in the International Settlement established by the British and Americans in 1863, reminiscent of the Canton factories. Among the many Scots in Shanghai (sometimes called the Shanghailanders!) most were employed in the business or manufacturing worlds. There were also some

Sculling Regatta at the Shanghai Bund by a Chinese artist. The Shanghai waterfront is always known as the Bund, from the Urdu word for quay.

Chests of tea being shipped downriver to the coast.

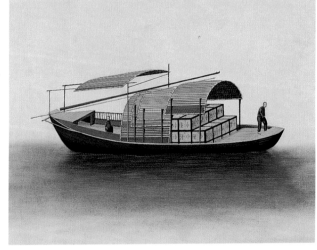

The Shanghai Bund in 1927. The domed building in the centre is the Hongkong and Shanghai Bank. The office of Jardine Matheson and Co is the building with columns second from the right.

Scottish oddbods: one, in the Bubbling Well area of the city, ran a country tea-shack where nostalgic expatriates 'would sit in the garden and enjoy home baked scones and goats-milk cream cheese and other delicious goodies'.

Although as a trading port Shanghai got off to a faster start than Hong Kong, the colony ceded by the Treaty of Nanjing, Shanghai's later success as a textile-producing centre was to be one of the causes of Hong Kong's booming success in the 1950s. With the Communist takeover of China in 1949, a huge number of Shanghai textile manufacturers and shipping magnates fled to Hong Kong where, with Chinese entrepreneurial skill, they quickly built new empires.

5
Hong Kong grows

If Shanghai was the hare in the second half of the nineteenth century and the beginning of the twentieth, Hong Kong was the tortoise. Although Robert Fortune was greatly enamoured by the bay of Hong Kong in the 1840s, 'one of the finest which I have ever seen', he was altogether pessimistic about the new colony: 'I fear Hong-kong will be a failure'. By the late 1860s John Thomson was still, as Fortune had been, critical of the high crime rate, caused, in his opinion, by the Chinese 'passion for gambling'. Thomson identified gambling as the root of crime, but he was close to pinpointing its affinities with enterprise and success. Of the Chinese traders he said 'They are certainly very enterprising', and he was astounded by the number of respectable gamblers: 'I should hardly have been more amazed had I beheld an elder of the Scotch kirk cautiously staking his savings after church hours on Sunday'.

The enterprising approach of the Chinese 'shopkeepers, tradesmen, servants, boat-people, and Coolies' in Hong Kong is reminiscent of the assistance given by the local Chinese to the Portuguese in Macau in the sixteenth century. Just as Macau owed part of its success as a trading port to the amicable relationship between the Portuguese traders and the Chinese food suppliers and shipbuilders, so Hong Kong was to grow with similar assistance. Thomson may have felt that 'Europeans in Hongkong live in a very expensive style' but he did not fail to notice that it was the Chinese who provided the sedan chairs, the stalls selling 'preserved European provisions . . . fruit, fish, and so forth', and the building workforce.

Back home the British government complained about the sluggishness of trade in Hong Kong, the expense of the colony and its succession of inappropriate and inefficient governors. Hong Kong had been intended to be another Canton. This was not to be. In Canton, trade had been predominantly one-sided, with minimal Chinese interference and a multitude of restrictions. In Hong Kong things were different: both British and Chinese worked together towards its success, with greater freedom.

The majority of Chinese in Hong Kong, like the Europeans, were newcomers, some of them English-speakers from the British settlements of Malacca and Singapore who were more enterprising under British rule than the few original Chinese inhabitants. Among the British were a number of Scots, many of whom helped to lay the foundations of Hong Kong's territory and institutions. These included not only Hong Kong's

Hong Kong street life was dominated by the Chinese, as depicted by Count Emanuel Andrasy in 1859 (detail).

Jardine Matheson and Co's executive house and godowns at North Point, Hong Kong, with Kellet Island to the left, painted by a Chinese artist about 1855.

'founding fathers', William Jardine and James Matheson, but also colonial servants, bankers, engineers, and military and medical men.

Jardine Matheson was the first company to build up warehouses and offices in Hong Kong, at the eastern end of the harbour, now North Point. Opium continued to be the chief import to China, silk the chief export, as little tea made its way to Hong Kong. Tea was exported from the treaty ports, mainly Fuzhou and Shanghai. In Shanghai Jardine Matheson built up a large office and was known as the Princely Hong.

The family solidarity of Jardine Matheson and Co is quite remarkable, the company still headed by members of the Keswick family, descendants of William Jardine's sister. Many of the Jardine family hailed from, and retired to, southwest Scotland, to houses not unlike the Number One house in Hong Kong. Perhaps this family closeness accounts for the enormous respect the Chinese had for the company, which bore comparison with a Chinese family-run business. Jardine's certainly attracted some of the most enterprising Chinese compradores. Derived from the Portuguese word meaning a buyer, a compradore was precisely this: he was the Chinese buyer or agent acting for a European firm and he took the place that had previously been held in Canton trading days by the Chinese *hong* merchants, those Mowquas, Tenquas and Howquas who had acted for the East India Company traders. The compradore was a new breed, however, with new freedom: he not only acted as middleman between European and Chinese businesses, but in many cases he used his entrepreneurial flair to build up his own trading firm.

One such compradore who was to stand at the head of a multi-generation family of compradores (similar to the Jardine empire) was Robert Ho Tung. Although of Eurasian birth, Robert Ho Tung chose to claim Chinese nationality, but his education in English gave him a head start in his dealings with the British community in Hong Kong. One of the first Chinese to adopt a Western Christian name, Robert Ho Tung joined Jardine Matheson and Co in 1880 as shipping office clerk, rising to the position of chief compradore for the firm in Hong Kong by 1883. In his own right he eventually became director of eighteen companies on the China coast and owner of vast real estate holdings. His links with Scotland were to extend from business to family, as he was to marry Clara Maclean, the daughter of a Jardine Matheson partner, Alexander Campbell Maclean. And Ho family links with Britain have perpetuated: the refurbishment of the gallery of oriental antiquities at the British Museum was made possible by Sir Robert's grandson, Sir Joseph Hotung, after whom the gallery is named.

The Ho family: at the centre Sir Robert Ho Tung, flanked by Lady Clara and Lady Margaret Ho Tung. Immediately behind them are three of Sir Robert's sons: Edward, at the right, was compradore for the Hongkong and Shanghai Bank.

Sir Thomas Sutherland, founder of the Hongkong and Shanghai Bank. Painting by Robert Swan, 1964, based on an original by J S Sargent, 1898.

It was not only the firm of Jardine Matheson and Co which was to employ the Ho family as compradores. The compradores of another of Hong Kong's great institutions, the Hongkong and Shanghai Banking Company, were headed by one of Sir Robert's sons, Edward Ho Tung, for over thirty years. And this great institution was also the brainchild of a Scot, Thomas Sutherland, who showed immense entrepreneurial nerve. Until the 1860s trade with China had been financed chiefly by agents such as Jardine's and Dent's, but the need for a bank to serve both traders and the Hong Kong government, with its costly road, dock and building schemes, was becoming evident.

The story goes that Thomas Sutherland, an employee of the Peninsular and Oriental Steamship Company, was relaxing with a copy of *Blackwood's Magazine*, a Scottish periodical, aboard a small P&O steamer en route from Hong Kong to Shantou. An article on banking prompted him to ponder that 'one of the very simplest things in the world would be to start a bank in China more or less founded upon Scottish principles'. It was not long until that opportunity arose.

Several months later Sutherland was informed that the Bombay-based Royal Bank of China was about to move into China to mop up the profits of the China trade. Incensed that the Chinese should be so 'unpatriotic' as to 'submit to a Bombay enterprise', Sutherland that very evening wrote his prospectus for a bank. Within a few weeks, with a capital of five million dollars and a provisional committee of fifteen, the Hongkong and Shanghai Bank was launched in March 1865. Sutherland had moved just in time: having secured the financial and moral support of almost all the leading firms in Hong Kong, he had ousted his potential rival and the Bombay bank was forced to

Oil painting of Hong Kong by a Chinese artist. As John Thomson wrote in 1868, the city of Victoria 'rears its granite buildings, like the side of a richly-sculpted pyramid'. Note also the variety of vessels in the harbour.

close. Although he was to leave Hong Kong shortly afterwards, in 1867, Sutherland had laid the founding principles upon which the Bank was to flourish: the support of leading local traders and the Hong Kong government. He had also seen the establishment in 1866 of the Hong Kong Mint. This made Hong Kong silver dollars, the replacement for the other forms of silver that had been the common trading currency until then.

The financial stability provided by the Bank was timely, as Hong Kong was expanding. By 1851 there were about 30,000 Chinese and 1500 people of other nationalities, building progress was being made and roads constructed, many of them under the direction of Scottish engineers such as Murdoch Bruce. The area of Hong Kong was increasing also: in 1860 the strip of land on the mainland, known as Kowloon, directly opposite the city of Victoria, was ceded to the British.

One of the most insistent advocates of the necessity to annex Kowloon had been General James Hope Grant, who considered it 'essential to the defence of Hong Kong harbour and the town of Victoria'. Hope Grant was one of the many Scottish military men who played major parts in the military encounters between the British and the Chinese in the attempt to improve trading relations. Hailing from Kilgraston in Perthshire, Grant was often said to be a better cellist than reader of maps and compasses,

General Sir James Hope Grant painted by his brother Sir Francis Grant in the 1850s.

but he was a popular figure with 'a quiet simplicity and kindliness about his manner'. He had fought in the first Anglo-Chinese war of 1839 to 1842 which had resulted in the cession of Hong Kong, and he returned to China in 1860 to participate in the final stages of the second Anglo-Chinese war.

The official cession of Kowloon was only one small part of what Hope Grant's contemporaries Lord Elgin and Harry Parkes sought from the Chinese emperor in Beijing in 1860. Essentially they wanted to ratify the Treaty of Tianjin, which had been signed in 1858 in an attempt to improve trading relations with China. With military backup from British forces under Hope Grant and with the support of French forces, they headed for Beijing, where official negotiations took a bad turn. Although Elgin and Parkes survived, a number of the British party were imprisoned in the emperor's Summer Palace, just outside Beijing, and killed by the Chinese. The French and British troops retaliated by looting and burning the Summer Palace, behaviour that appalled Hope Grant. A vast quantity of looted imperial treasures nevertheless found its way out of China at the time. These were to cause a sensation amongst appreciative Western connoisseurs whose knowledge of Chinese art had previously been limited almost entirely to the Chinese knick-knacks made specifically for the west.

The task was left to Hope Grant and Lord Elgin to face the emperor's brother, Prince Gong, who had been given charge of foreign relations, to demand the signing of the convention. As Hope Grant wrote, the prince was 'pale as death . . . expecting every moment to have his head blown off by the infernal machine opposite him'. But 'the whole business went off satisfactorily' and by the

James Stewart Lockhart in the garden of a Chinese official.

Convention of Beijing of 1860 Kowloon was ceded to the British, and several new ports were opened to trade (Tianjin, four towns on the Yangzi River as far west as Hankou, and the island now known as Taiwan). Missionaries were to be permitted greater freedom to travel in China, and the British were to be allowed a representative in Beijing.

Almost forty years later another Scot was to be involved in the further expansion of Hong Kong. The much-debated 99-year lease of the mainland area beyond Kowloon, together with a number of islands, collectively known as the New Territories, was signed on 30 June 1898. The task of agreeing precise boundaries and hoisting the flag was given to James Haldane Stewart Lockhart.

Stewart Lockhart was born in Argyllshire in 1858 and educated in Edinburgh before being appointed a cadet to Hong Kong in 1878. This entailed studying Chinese in

London for a year and working in the Colonial Office. By 1879 he arrived in Hong Kong, furthering his studies of Chinese and beginning to collect Chinese art and coins. His years in the colonial service proved him a highly competent linguist, administrator and scholar, all skills which endeared him to the Chinese. Indeed he became a great friend of Robert Ho Tung and guardian to one of his sons, Ho Sai Lai.

At the time of the leasing of the New Territories Lockhart was both Colonial Secretary (the governor's right-hand man) and Registrar General. At the same time Japanese encroachment in northern China had instigated a European scramble to acquire footholds in China. Not only did Britain lease the New Territories of Hong Kong in 1898, but she also acquired a similar-sized area on the northeast coast of China called Weihaiwei, now simply Weihai.

Stewart Lockhart must have been disappointed never to have been appointed governor of Hong Kong, but he did become the first civil commissioner of Weihaiwei. For Lockhart here was an opportunity to use his administrative and linguistic skills to build up a northern Chinese version of Hong Kong and develop its trade in groundnuts, oil, silk and salt. In this he was helped by his great friend and fellow Scot, Reginald Johnston, who had arrived in Hong Kong in 1898 and followed a path similar to that of Stewart Lockhart. Both men put tremendous energy and enthusiasm into Weihaiwei, but their vision did not materialize perhaps because both were really scholars at heart. Certainly Johnston was a prolific writer on China and an intrepid traveller, and in 1919 accepted the post of European tutor to the young puppet emperor Puyi in the Forbidden City in Beijing. The post had first been offered to Lockhart who had turned it down, knowing that Johnston would be the better incumbent. Lockhart was eventually defeated by lack of funding and facilities in Weihaiwei, and retired in 1921, after nineteen years' service there. Chinese research continued to occupy him in London until his death in 1937, when he left his collection of Chinese art and artefacts to his former school in Edinburgh, George Watson's College.

Lockhart Road, named after Stewart Lockhart, home of Hong Kong's nightclubs.

The monkey's joyful cry of 'Wei-Hai-Wei!!!' in this soap advertisement of 1898, the year in which Weihaiwei became a British colony, points to the impact of the event.

GOOD FOR CHINA! "WEI-HAI-WEI!!!"

Reginald Johnston in Beijing, possibly in the Forbidden City where he taught the puppet emperor Puyi.

Johnston died a year later, having returned first to Weihaiwei as the last British commissioner, handing back the colony to China in 1930 after thirty-two years of colonial rule. He returned to England to become professor of Chinese at the School of Oriental Studies at the University of London.

It would seem strange to leave Hong Kong without mention of at least one or two Scottish medical men, who have played such a major role in the story of the China trade so far. Dr Thomas Boswall Watson has already cropped up in connection with his friend and fellow sketcher, William Melrose, but he was to leave his mark in Hong Kong as the founder of the Watson chain of chemists, still in existence today.

Also still operating successfully today is Hong Kong's first company to make dairy products: Dairy Farm. This was founded by Patrick Manson, a medical graduate of the University of Aberdeen, and a man with such a passion for insects that he was to acquire the nickname 'Mosquito Manson'. Mosquitoes had certainly preoccupied Manson during his years in China from 1867 to 1883 before he moved to Hong Kong to set up a private medical practice. With his interest in hygiene and tropical medicine, Manson was appalled at some of the practices of the otherwise often most fastidious Chinese. He saw pigsties on the first, second and third floors of houses, he saw calves driven into basements to provide milk for Europeans, and he saw the same cows later slaughtered and dismembered in these basements because they had grown too big to be got out.

Manson's first move was to establish a college of medicine in Hong Kong to improve the colony's medical services. His next was to set up a dairy farm because 'From a hygienic point of view the milk supply of a community

An expatriate beach party in Hong Kong. Note the river steam boat being used as a pleasure boat.

is second only in importance to its water supply'. Initial problems of making 'exotic' cows happy in the subtropics with the right kind of grass and terrain were eventually overcome and in 1889 Manson was able to leave Hong Kong, satisfied that Dairy Farm was producing almost sterile milk. Although at that time the milk was mainly for the European community in Hong Kong, as dairy produce was alien to the Chinese diet, in recent years many Hong Kong Chinese have come to accept milk and, to a lesser extent, cheese. Manson can therefore be regarded as the pioneer of dairy products amongst the Hong Kong Chinese. On return to London Manson took up the post of medical adviser to the Colonial Office and founded the London School of Hygiene and Tropical Medicine.

Hong Kong was full of Scots in many walks of life. It still is. And just as Scots at home like to subdivide and consider themselves as members of their individual clans, so Scots abroad tend to adopt this clan attitude and form themselves into a group proud of its homeland. Such sentiments led to the founding in 1881 of the St Andrews Society.

St Andrews Day was celebrated in style, particularly in Hong Kong and Shanghai, where a special horseracing meeting would be held, enlivened by the Scottish airs played by pipers and drummers. In Shanghai the participant who came last in the Jardine's race was presented with a gigantic wooden spoon which would be duly filled with whisky

Thistles, kilts and tartan sashes: Caledonian Ball in Hankou in the 1930s.

and passed round all the staff. The evening would see the crowning event, the annual Caledonian Ball, in a hall decorated with blue and white banners, thistle motifs and heather, and clan shields and flags, the president's table draped with a huge St Andrew's flag. Kilts and sporrans would be donned, and ladies' frocks would sport tartan sashes and ribbons. An evening of Scottish reels and the presentation of the debutantes, each with a bouquet fastened with blue and white ribbon and a thistle brooch, would be concluded by the traditional procession of the haggis, borne aloft and guarded by drawn sword. Whisky would have been an absolute necessity on such occasions, and the Scots had not ignored this. In 1884, three years after the founding of the St Andrews Society, Eaton John Caldbeck and John Macgregor took over a wine and spirits business which had begun in Shanghai in 1864. Within the next thirty years Caldbeck Macgregor and Co was to expand into the largest business of its kind in the east.

These are just a few of the Scots who helped to lay the foundations of Hong Kong and establish better trading relations with China. Another book needs to be written to recount the lives of the many thousands more who have contributed to the development of Hong Kong and China throughout the twentieth century, a century in which China has experienced vast political upheavals and there have been two world wars.

The twentieth century has seen a change of emphasis in the west's relationship with China: trading has been augmented by assisting China to develop her manufacturing businesses. By the beginning of the century companies such as Jardine Matheson and Co had diversified to provide practical assistance to the Chinese. They helped develop their textile industry, their shipping, their railways, their mines, and even established a brewery in Shanghai. From China they exported goods such as hides, oils, bristles, egg products and beans in exchange for cotton textiles, chemicals, machinery and opium, the import of opium being finally banned in 1945. Hong Kong's main function was as a re-export centre for goods made in China, although it developed its own manufacturing businesses from the 1950s with the influx of mainland Chinese, many from Shanghai.

Britain has also benefited from an influx of Chinese: almost every small town, even in remote parts of Scotland, has a Chinese restaurant or takeaway owned by a Hong Kong Cantonese who has grasped the opportunity for business. That the Cantonese have had this opportunity is due to the success of Hong Kong as a British colony, which, in its turn, would have come to nothing without the help of the Cantonese. Over the last decade however Hong Kong has once again become dependent on China with the phenomenal growth of Shenzhen nearby, which now manufactures many of the goods previously made in Hong Kong.

Scotland's present-day imports from China and Hong Kong – cashmere, children's toys, stationery, clothing and jewellery – reflect China's adaptability to the needs of the west. Recent Chinese investment in the manufacture of electrical components and televisions in Scotland indicates a confidence in those practical skills that have been the hallmark of Scotland's contribution to China and Hong Kong. Scotland continues to furnish China and Hong Kong with businessmen, financiers, engineers and doctors, as well as with engineering and telecommunications equipment, whisky and doubledecker buses.

James Stewart Lockhart was not thinking of 1997 when he hoisted the British flag at the boundary between China and the New Territories of Hong Kong in 1898, thereby formalizing the 99-year lease of the colony. Now in 1997 it is difficult to cease making the distinction between Hong Kong and China. Yet both are now China. In some ways we have come full circle. China is now once again, as it was in the early days of trade, reliant on itself to organize its trade with the rest of the world. We must remain confident that it will succeed. It certainly has the resources.

6
Scotland's response

So, what has been Scotland's response to the China trade? How has the China trade affected the arts and daily life in Scotland?

Anything made in Europe in Chinese style – or what the maker *thought* was a Chinese or even oriental style – is usually described as chinoiserie. Rather sadly Scotland has been little touched by the waves of chinoiserie that have swept through Europe from the late seventeenth century to the present day. Scotland has no great quantities of Chinese-patterned earthenware and porcelain, no surviving Chinese-style garden pavilions and pagodas, no Brighton Pavilion, and little Chinese-style furniture: no Chelsea, no Chambers, no Chippendale.

Not that Scotland produced no chinoiserie at all. There is some, most of it rather later than much of the European chinoiserie, and there may well be more lying unnoticed and awaiting discovery in houses and gardens throughout Scotland.

Scotland was not slow to follow England in the production of pottery. The potteries of Chelsea, Bristol and Liverpool got going in the 1740s, those of Glasgow and the east coast of Scotland in the late 1740s and the 1750s. The impetus may have come from England, but it may equally have come from the Netherlands, which, as we have seen, had such strong trading links with Scotland. The Dutch had been producing blue and white ware since the early seventeenth century, mainly at Delft, in imitation of the blue and white porcelain they were importing from China through the Dutch East India Company. A hint that Scotland's early

Wemyss ware vase made about 1880.

The Chinese drawing room of an Edinburgh house painted by Barbara Liaudinski in 1991, a supreme example of contemporary chinoiserie.

The pagoda in Kew Gardens, designed by William Chambers in 1761-2.

pottery manufacturing inspiration came from the Netherlands lies in the name of Scotland's first pottery, the Delftfield Pottery in Glasgow. Delftfield produced pottery with freely painted blue and white decoration, including the splendid Saracen's Head Inn punchbowl with its curious version of the Glasgow coat of arms and a Chinese-style meandering floral border. The inspiration may be only secondhand Chinese through the Netherlands, but it is certainly there. Similar inspiration can be seen in the blue and white wares produced by the Prestonpans and West Pans potteries near Edinburgh at the end of the eighteenth century.

The next wave of Scottish pottery with chinoiserie designs came in the second half of the nineteenth century. The source of the Chinese gentlemen among bamboo on the Wemyss ware panelled vase, dating from about 1880, may not be a Chinese design, but perhaps a Meissen porcelain vase from the collection at Wemyss Castle from which the pottery designers gleaned many of the designs for their boldly painted wares. Of more obviously direct Chinese inspiration are the designs on the roughly contemporaneous transfer-printed pottery of J and M P Bell of Glasgow. The dragons, pagodas and Chinese fairytales that decorate the enormous variety of wares produced at the Bells' Glasgow Pottery have obvious sources such as the Temple of Heaven in Beijing and the Chinese play *The Romance of the Western Chamber*. Although it has been said that these were 'specially designed by Chinese artists', this has not been proven. What has been proven beyond doubt by finds of Bells' ware all over the Far East is that much of this ware was exported to the Far East. This phenomenon of the apparent reversal of the porcelain trade is one that has yet to be explained.

Plate and punchbowl made in the 1880s and 1890s by J and M P Bell's Glasgow Pottery with transfer-printed Chinese-style designs.

Chinoiserie is perhaps most obvious in the many European imitations of Chinese porcelain. This is hardly surprising considering that Europe's earliest conception of Chinese pattern and ornament was gained mainly from imported Chinese blue and white porcelain. The freely painted Chinese landscapes with pagodas and bridges – of the sort that inspired the ubiquitous Willow Pattern, first produced at Caughley in England in 1780 – may also have been the inspiration behind the Chinese-style garden pavilions and bridges which began to grace the more informal parks of Britain and Europe in the 1740s and 1750s.

Responsible for some of these was William Chambers, later architect to George III and the first European architect to go to China and make extensive drawings of Chinese buildings. And here we have a tenuous connection with Scotland, because Chambers was of Scottish ancestry. His parents however had moved to Gothenburg where they worked for the Swedish East India Company, probably alongside other Scotsmen such as Charles Irvine and Colin Campbell. William likewise was to begin his career in the services of the company, travelling to Canton in 1743 and 1748, latterly as supercargo. This position would have permitted him access to the factory area of Canton from where he would at least have caught glimpses of Chinese architecture. Although Chambers' *Designs of Chinese Buildings, Furniture, Dresses, Machines, and Utensils . . .*, published in 1757, contains no precise drawing for the pagoda that he designed for the royal gardens at Kew in 1761-2, and despite doubts that Chambers ever really studied Chinese architecture in the flesh, a comparison of the pagoda, which still stands today, with, for example, the painting of one of Canton's pagodas on James Drummond's wall-paper suggests very strongly that Chambers did take a first-hand scholarly approach to Chinese design rather than the more frivolous one adopted by porcelain painters and

Designs for Chinese-style night nursery furniture by John Murray of Whytock and Reid, Edinburgh. Compare the hump-backed stretchers, the use of medallions on the cot, and the horse-hoof feet with the Chinese table opposite.

Cockpen chair made by Whytock and Reid, Edinburgh, in the 1920s. Note the trellis-work back, reminiscent of Chinese garden fencing, and the Chinese-style hump-backed top rail.

garden designers. That Chambers' chinoiserie did not extend as far north as his Scottish architectural triumphs of Dundas House and Duddingston House in Edinburgh is a great pity. Documentary evidence however suggests that the Scottish estates of Inveraray, Blair, Dunkeld and Taymouth all had Chinese-style buildings, bridges or railings, designed in the mid-eighteenth century, but none have survived.

Twentieth-century designers who adopted a scholarly approach similar to that of Chambers, but this time to the design of furniture and interiors, were William Simpson and John Murray. Simpson joined the Edinburgh firm of Whytock and Reid, which specialized in furniture and interior design, in 1892, and was to run the design office for almost fifty years. During that time much of the Whytock and Reid furniture displays Chinese elements, many of them faithful copies of Chinese designs. Not only individual pieces, but whole rooms such as the Overdale nursery, would follow a Chinese theme. By the 1930s the company had established more direct links with China. Through a family connection they had carpets of their own design manufactured in Beijing, and acted as agents in the sale of Chinese antiquities acquired by an enterprising British railway engineer in Beijing.

Even today Chinese arts and crafts continue to exert an influence on a small number of Scottish artists and craftsmen. Interior designers and furniture painters such as Barbara Liaudinski have created complete Chinese-style rooms which may appear wildly eccentric yet have a firm basis in scholarship. The potter Sarah-Jane Selwood, while reluctant to say she is directly influenced by Chinese pottery and porcelain, admits that it would be hard to ignore the achievements of the Chinese potter. Her pieces

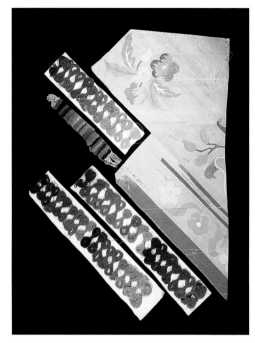

Whytock and Reid sent wool colour swatches and annotated painted designs to the manufacturer of their carpets in China.

Typical Chinese table with hump-backed stretchers and decorative medallions.

White beaked porcelain bowl by Sarah-Jane Selwood, Edinburgh 1996.

exhibit a purity reminiscent of early Chinese monochrome porcelain. Textile designers, too, have learned much from the Chinese: Norma Starszakowna has exhibited her work in China and is involved with the Chinese in developing wax resist textiles.

Perhaps the small amount of chinoiserie in Scotland is but a reflection of the main thrust of Scotland's involvement in the China trade: the involvement in the practical sides of the trade, the medicinal drugs, the tea, the plants. These have certainly left their mark in Scotland. The import of rhubarb root led to Scotland's rhubarb-growing craze and the making of patent medicines such as Gregory's Powder. The tea trade encouraged Scottish silversmiths and then potters to make equipment for the tea table, it stimulated Scotland's shipbuilding industry, and it has left us with some of its oldest merchants still in existence: Melrose's in Edinburgh, Matthew Algie in Glasgow and Braithwaite's in Dundee. Chinese plants, particularly rhododendrons and woodland plants, have transformed our gardens and

Scottish silversmiths were quick to react to the new vogue for tea drinking in the early 18th century. This so-called bullet teapot was made by James Ker in 1725-6.

Braithwaite's the tea merchant in Dundee still contains the original shop fittings of the late 1860s.

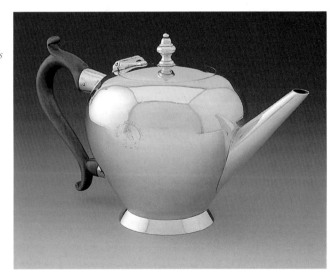

encouraged plant collectors from the Royal Botanic Garden in Edinburgh to return to China with their plastic bags to seek new species. A stroll through the Garden today reveals a hillside devoted to Chinese plants which can be viewed from a Chinese-style pavilion and bridge. Such a prospect may just inspire the adventurous Scots of today to go and see the real thing.

Hong Kong 1996. If given the go-ahead, an 88-storey skyscraper on the waterfront will rise well above the Peak.

Further reading

AIRLIE, Shiona. *Thistle and Bamboo: the life and times of Sir James Stewart Lockhart*. Oxford 1989.

CLUNAS, Craig (ed). *Chinese Export Art and Design*. London 1987.

COATES, Austin. *A Macao Narrative*. Hong Kong 1978.

COATS, Alice M. *Garden Shrubs and their Histories*. London 1963.

COATS, Alice M. *The Plant Hunters*. New York, St Louis and San Francisco 1969.

CONNER, Patrick. *The China Trade 1600-1860*. Brighton 1986.

CROSSMAN, Carl L. *The Decorative Arts of the China Trade*. Suffolk 1991.

FORREST, Denys. *Tea for the British*. London 1973.

FORTUNE, Robert. *Three Years' Wanderings in China*. First edition London 1847, paperback London 1987.

FORTUNE, Robert. *A Journey to the Tea Countries of China*. First edition London 1852, paperback London 1987.

FORTUNE, Robert. *A Residence among the Chinese . . . from 1853-1856*. London 1857.

FOUST, Clifford M. *Rhubarb: the wondrous drug*. Princeton 1992.

HAW, Stephen G. *A Traveller's History of China*. Moreton-in-Marsh 1995.

HIBBERT, Christopher. *The Dragon Wakes: China and the West 1793-1911*. London 1970.

HOBHOUSE, Henry. *Seeds of Change: five plants that transformed mankind*. London 1985.

HOWARD, David S. *A Tale of Three Cities: Canton, Shanghai and Hong Kong*. London 1997.

JORG, C J A. *Porcelain and the Dutch China Trade*. The Hague 1982.

KEAY, John. *The Honourable Company: a history of the English East India Company*. London 1991.

KESWICK, Maggie (ed). *The Thistle and the Jade: a celebration of 150 years of Jardine, Matheson and Co.* London 1982.

MACGREGOR, David R. *The Tea Clippers*. Conway Maritime Press, n.p. 1972.

MO, Timothy. *An Insular Possession*. London 1986.

MUI, Hoh-cheung and Mui, Lorna (eds). *William Melrose in China 1845-1855: the letters of a Scottish tea merchant*. Edinburgh 1973.

OVENDEN, Richard. *John Thomson (1837-1921): photographer*. Edinburgh 1997.

PORTAL, Jane. 'Luxuries for Trade' in *The British Museum Book of Chinese Art,* ed. Jessica Rawson. London 1992.

SERGEANT, Harriet. *Shanghai*. London 1991.

SMOUT, T C. *Scottish Trade on the Eve of Union 1660-1707*. Edinburgh and London 1963.

STEAD sisters. *Stone-Paper-Scissors: Shanghai 1921-45*. Chipping Norton 1991.

WELSH, Frank. *A History of Hong Kong*. London 1994.

WILSON, C Anne. *Food and Drink in Britain*. London 1973.

Acknowledgements

Anthony Butler: 19; Boots Company Archive: 19 top; Early Technology: 86; Education Board of the Merchant Company of Edinburgh and the School Governing Council of George Watson's College: 75, 79, 82, 83; Martyn Gregory : frontispiece, 10 bottom, 24, 34, 51 top; HSBC Holdings plc: 6, 20, 70 top, 72, 76, 77; Susan Leiper: 7, 9, 27, 46, 47, 57, 88, 89 right; Keith Macgregor: 94; Matheson and Co Ltd: 40, 43 bottom; Beatrice Morton: 66 right; National Library of Scotland: 12, 41 left, 44 top, 51 bottom, 52, 55, 69; National Maritime Museum London: 10 top, 59; National Museums of Scotland: cover, 16, 19 bottom, 22, 26, 28, 29, 30, 32, 33 left, 35, 36, 38, 43 top, 44 bottom, 49, 53, 54 top, 56, 58, 63 bottom, 64, 70 bottom, 81, 87, 89 left, 91 bottom, 92 bottom; NMS courtesy J Allan Braithwaite: 93, 96; NMS courtesy Matthew Algie: 33 right; NMS courtesy Mayway (UK) Ltd: 17; NMS courtesy Melrose's Tea: 25, 45, 48, 50, 54 bottom, 62, 63 top; NMS courtesy Beatrice Morton: 66 left; NMS courtesy Royal Pharmaceutical Society of Great Britain, Scottish Department: 18; NMS courtesy Whytock and Reid: 90, 91 top; Robert Nield: 80; Private collections: 31, 37; Daphne Robson: 84; Royal Botanic Garden Edinburgh: 15, 65; Royal Horticultural Society, Lindley Library: 61; Scottish National Portrait Gallery: 78; Sarah-Jane Selwood: 92 top; Sze Yuan Tang Collection: 74; University of Edinburgh, Centre for the Study of Christianity in the Non-Western World: 67, 68.

Purely fanciful chinoiserie Chinamen used by Braithwaite's as an advertisement.